Praise for
COLLECTED POEMS

"[Ellen Bryant Voigt] aligns herself firmly within the pastoral tradition, following in a direct line behind the likes of Virgil, Clare, Edward Thomas, and especially the darker side of Frost. Like them, she doesn't apotheosize nature. She knows all too well the travails and tedium of rural life, but also knows its consolations."
—David Wojahn, *On the Sea Wall*

"Even for a reader who knows [Voigt's] individual books well, reading straight through the volume is newly exhilarating. There are enduring consistencies in this poet's work across the years, both in subject matter and style: a distinctive austerity of manner that never sounds detached and a quietly spectacular precision."
—Jim Schley, *Seven Days*

"These poems, collected from eight books dating back to 1976, establish Voigt as one of the most proficient and accomplished poets writing today. Infusing narrative with lyric power, these precise, yet visceral entries engage with ordinary people in their strangeness, as well as with animals domesticated and wild. . . . [E]ach poem achieves, through earned emotion and vision, broader impact. A trained pianist since childhood, Voigt is a musician at heart and a formalist who rarely works in received forms. This rewarding and expansive work does justice to her commendable vision and ear."
—*Publishers Weekly*, starred review

Praise for Ellen Bryant Voigt

"Reading Voigt one comes to understand that what we think of as reality is the product of both painstaking observation and imagination. . . . She favors a language that is both precise and lush, and a narrative that is both immediately accessible and richly layered with meaning."
—Charles Simic, *New York Review of Books*

"Voigt has a highly tempered poetic intelligence, most obvious in her line by line determination to align evocative images with their emotional incentives."
—Sven Birkerts, *New York Times Book Review*

"[Voigt is a] genius. She is a poet of knowledge, and knowledge in the living, messy world."
—Robert Pinsky, *Washington Post Book World*

"Ellen Bryant Voigt has fashioned an art of passionate gravity and opulent music, an art at once ravishing and stern and deeply human."
—Academy Award in Literature citation,
American Academy of Arts and Letters

"The beauty and intensity of Ellen Bryant Voigt's sustained elegy leaves us feeling much as we do after listening to Mozart's *Requiem*: grief-stricken, transformed, and exalted."
—Francine Prose

"Voigt's poems are shorn of superfluity, each line shaved down to its essential, burning core. She is a poet of control and precision; across decades and amid differing poetical movements, Voigt is steadfast in her adherence to a clear-eyed iambic elegy—an elegy defined most strikingly by her devotion to unsentimental self-interrogation and her equally unflinching assessments of public life."
—Martin Mitchell, *Poetry Daily*

COLLECTED POEMS

ALSO BY ELLEN BRYANT VOIGT

POETRY

Claiming Kin

The Forces of Plenty

The Lotus Flowers

Two Trees

Kyrie

Shadow of Heaven

Messenger: New and Selected Poems, 1976–2006

Headwaters

PROSE

The Flexible Lyric

The Art of Syntax: Rhythm of Speech, Rhythm of Song

COLLECTED POEMS

Ellen Bryant Voigt

W. W. NORTON & COMPANY
Independent Publishers Since 1923

For information about permission to reproduce selections from this book, write to Permissions, W. W. Norton & Company, Inc., 500 Fifth Avenue, New York, NY 10110

For information about special discounts for bulk purchases, please contact W. W. Norton Special Sales at specialsales@wwnorton.com or 800-233-4830

Manufacturing by Lakeside Book Company
Book design by Chris Welch Design
Production manager: Julia Druskin

Library of Congress Control Number: 2024934149

ISBN 978-1-324-07624-7 pbk.

W. W. Norton & Company, Inc., 500 Fifth Avenue, New York, N.Y. 10110
www.wwnorton.com

W. W. Norton & Company Ltd., 15 Carlisle Street, London W1D 3BS

1 2 3 4 5 6 7 8 9 0

For my students,
from whom I learned so much.

CONTENTS

II

III

THE FORCES OF PLENTY (1983) 65

I

II

III

THE LOTUS FLOWERS (1987)

I

II

CLAIMING KIN

(1976)

For my family

I

Tropics

In the still morning when you move
toward me in sleep, for love,
I dream of

an island where long-stemmed cranes,
serious weather vanes,
turn slowly on one

foot. There the dragonfly folds
his mica wings and rides
the tall reed

close as a handle. The hippo yawns,
nods to thick pythons,
slack and drowsy, who droop down

like untied sashes
from the trees. The brash
hyenas do not cackle

and run but lie with their paws
on their heads like dogs.
The lazy crow's caw

falls like a sigh. In the field
below, the fat moles build
their dull passage with an old

instinct that needs
no light or waking; its slow beat
turns the hand in sleep

as we turn toward each other
in the ripe air of summer,
before the change of weather,

before the heavy drop
of the apples.

At the Edge of Winter

Vacant cornstalks rattle in the field;
the ditches are clogged with wet leaves.
Under the balding maple, toadstools
cluster like villages; their ruffled
undersides are brown. Inside,
we prepare for children: the clean
linens, the perfumed loins,
the aphrodisiac are ready. The cat,
our pagan daughter, has brought
her offering—the half-eaten, headless
carcass of a rabbit; its bright guts
bloom on the back porch step.

Rich November! Under the stiff
brown grass, the earth's maw
is full of tulip bulbs, hyacinth
and crocus to mull and ripen
these long months in deep freeze.
This is our season of opulence.
Festive, extravagant,
we'll spend your creamy seed
like the feathered milkweed blowing open.

Smeared with rabbit blood like a pagan,
I hack down the last new shoots
of the rosebush and arrange a bed
of rose and red cedar to scent
the fertile wound of the rabbit, lying
open and ready, primed for the winding

sheet of snow and the restless track
of the gray creative worm.

Animal Study

The cat sleeps stretched out
like someone's fur piece or rolled up
warm as flannel. She can sleep outside
on a flat rock, full belly up, claws
pulled in, soft neck exposed.
She dreams of how she will slink
through tall grass without disturbing it
and discover there with her famous eyes
a rabbit for her pleasure or a mouse
whose rapid breathing gives it away.
Gently she will embrace it,
one arm around its shoulders,
the other moving gracefully to strike.
Or she thinks of the lovely birds, swooping
and gliding, and how she will leap up
higher and higher, over the clothesline,
her arms elastic and extending themselves forever.
And waking slowly is like coming home
to sit on a patterned rug and wash herself.
Exquisite, invulnerable—
like the spider spinning his shimmering filigree
or the clear mosaic of the snake's imperial head.

Black Widow

Heavy in her hammock, she makes
ready for mating. All black,
black love in the pit of her
eye, she lolls at the center,
a soft black flower.

Her lover rounds the corner,
he has directions, he knows
what he's after. Small & dapper,
he climbs the high wire.
His careful footwork strums
the chord of her lair.
Each step closer sends
her the message, she opens
for him like a cloud.

Done with her, he wakes
to her massive body & wants
out. But with his seed,
alas! he has lost his fleet
foot, his map to the maze.
The wires hum their report:
meat in the net. Her hulk
moves in black hunger
across the steel-ribbed snare.

The Heart Is the Target

Hunger drove you across
the savannah and into the rainy
forest, sweating for prey.
As if this heat were an ally;
as if desire were a weapon.

Now you have reached the densest
vegetation. The path behind you
has closed like a curtain of water.
You have come upwind of your quarry.
The birds, with their passionate
language, announce your arrival.

Flushed by the chase, you lounge
on a viny cushion. Above the belly's
salt-lick, your breasts thrust forward
their wine-soaked centers. You strip
to the waist—a wash of light
against the green canvas. Soon,

in a murmur of branches, a figure
approaches. He sights the white field,
aims for the left breast's two
concentric circles. Then the pull
of the dark, centripetal eye.

Delilah

It wasn't the money or their silly
political speeches. I planned it
long before they came to mince
and whimper into their spit-stained
beards. What would they know
of power? Such thin sticks for my
magnificent boar, swinging a jawbone,
smashing and driving—ah, Samson!
your loins' heat, the sweet weight
 of your thighs. . . . That I could tame,
outwit, be stronger than *that*, I teased
the secret out. And in the early
morning, while the Philistines
leered from the fringed curtain,
while the royal harlots swayed
in their tents like frail-stemmed
flowers, while laborious wives molded
the meal-cake, their bellies warped
with children and children clutching
their slack breasts—in that hour
of last darkness, dressed in satin
split to an oiled thigh, I drove
my whetted shears to your sprawled
heap and the manly seat of power.

Preparation

The Bone-man lives in a stucco
house. He ticks his heels

on the cold terrazzo floor.
He parks his ragtruck

in the yard, instructs his crew
on the white telephone.

I am training my dog
to attack the red-capped hunter

bearing his long package.
I am training the tethered jay

to cry out against
the killer who cracks the latch.

On the open map, the road
to my house bulges like a vein.

He takes a train, he rents
a car, he lurches in

with an open fly. Sweet Eve
was just the Farmer's Daughter,

he wooed her with a wormy apple.
He's a dirty joke, he's

always everybody's last
lover, he's a regular

can of worms—you wry Medusa,
I am a mongoose staring you down.

Snakeskin

Down on the porch, the blacksnake
sits like a thick fist.
His back is flexed and slick.
The wedge of his forehead turns
to the sun. He does not remember
the skin shucked in the attic,
the high branches of our family tree.

The moth will not recall the flannel
cocoon. The snail empties the endless
convolutions of its shell. Think
of the husk of the locust,
sewn like an ear to the elm.
How easily they leave old lives,
as an eager lover steps from the skirts
at her ankles.
              Sleep corrects memory:
the long sleep of bear and woodchuck,
the sleep of the sea,
the sleep of the wooden spool unwinding,
the sleep of snow, when houses lose
their angles and edges, the slow
sleep of no dreaming;
and we could rise up in new skins
to a full confusion of green,
to the slick stalks of grasses,
and the catalpa, that beany tree, offering
its great, white, aromatic promise.

Southern Artifact

Lue Cinda Prunty Stone, the paper says
you were alive last week at 103,
rocking in a cane-bottom chair,
your breasts in your lap
and your squat legs, solid as bedposts,
wrapped in cotton stockings.
But that was not you.
Long before you sweat in my mother's kitchen,
put up pickles in a crock,
swatted flies with a Sycamore switch,
before you delivered signs and blessings
to black children hunkered down beside you,
before your teeth rotted with snuff,
you had begun to seep away.
All that time you were rocking,
while you turned up to us a stupid, stoic face,

the runners were kneading the red dirt
into a mighty poultice
that slowly sucked you out of yourself,
and you went down into the earth—
willing yourself away without our notice—
until your eyes were only props,
the mouth's singing automatic.
All that was left, Lue Cinda,
When a host of relatives and friends
gathered in Gretna to bury you—
your face, your clothes, the chair, all
that was left was what we had created:

a piece of lore, our mother-lode
of tradition, our nigra mammy.
And if I undid your kerchief
your head would fragment
and the rank pieces of a region
fall quietly into your lap.

American at Auschwitz

1. NEAR CRACOW

Here, by the Vistula:
the stacks of bundled grain
established on the hillside—

how like small men,
heads bowing,
necks bent down by the heavy air,
the pounds of ashes
drifted across the river.
How sympathetic they seem,
morose, guilty. . . .

See.
The mind is fat with suppositions.

2. GUARD'S HOUSE

There is no irony
in the blossoms by the fences,
red geraniums flourishing
by the trellis
where once hung
frail Jewish flowers,
delicate vines
of arms and legs,
ribs like petals,

ready for plucking,
black eyes turning
toward the sun.
Why not accept coincidence—
some modest German gardener
who delighted in
planting, weeding out,
plowing under.

    3. SELECTION

History never repeats.
We must limit our vision.
We must not break and run
when we remember
the victims running,
naked, to their chambers,
their hands covering
their breasts as the nipples darken
the breasts darken
the skin is charred and
turns brown and then
black their hair is singed by
the heat it kinks and
curls it will not lie
still it springs up
on their heads their lips
peel back puff out blow up

their tongues swell in
their mouths their speech thickens
it slows down like molasses
the white guards are laughing
in white gowns they are laughing,
the dogs are showing
their white, ridiculous
teeth, and the late sky ripens
like a bruise.

Stork

There are seventeen species of stork.

The painted stork is pink in his nuptial plumage.

The milky stork woos with his large flat bill.

The marabou offers her carrion, as does the adjutant.

Due to irregular throat structure, storks have no voice;

they strike their beaks together in lovesong.

Newborns know to swallow the fish headfirst.

In the myth of the moon-bird, storks impregnate women.

All storks adhere to serial monogamy.

In the mating season, two species are migratory:

the black stork who roosts in platforms in the forests of Poland;

the familiar white stork ("good luck" in Western Europe).

They are surpassed in endurance by none but the arctic tern.

They travel a thousand miles to Africa.

They soar on the thermal current.

They precede the rainy season.

They carry the unborn in from the marshland.

If a stork nests in your chimney, a son will be born.

If a stork nests in your chimney, your house will be empty.

If a stork leaves the nest, that is an omen.

If a stork leaves the nest forever, disaster will strike the area.

If a stork's shadow falls on the rosebush, grief descends to the village.

If a stork is damaged, the weather darkens.

If you kill a stork, kinsmen surround you, clacking long sticks together
  like knives.

Suicides

Inkblot, sperm on a slide, a squirm
of minnows from the helicopter's
view, the whales have beached.
All day the volunteers have poked
and prodded, but they will not
turn back. Behind them their salty
element foams and rushes: how often
they sounded the dark layers,
past the lacy skeletons of coral,
the squid preparing his black cloak
for a getaway—the ease of gliding,
motion in the midst of motion,
through water! the pull of water
as they stored breath and dove again
and again, looking for bottom, down
to where fish blossom among the sponges
and fossils, where the plants are meat-
eating and sexual, where the ocean
opens to cold drafts that clamp
an iron vise against the skull.

Graceful in water, they labor now
toward palmetto and tufted
hillocks, the hot sun bleaching
and drying out. Their fins dig into
something solid, the broad flukes
spade, then anchor in the sand.

Dialogue: Poetics

1ST VOICE

Admiring the web, do we
forget the spider? The real
poem is a knife-edge,
quick and clean.

The bird needs
no extra feather, the stone
sits in its own shape.

Consider the weather.

We could say that snow
fills the crotches of the birch
and makes a webbed hand.

We could say,
Look at the graceful line
of falling snow!

The point is: It
falls and falls on trees
and houses, with or
without comment.

ITEM:
Should we record snow
falling on the tamaracks
beside the black Winooski
River, and not the trapper
crouched on the far bank,
who thinks: Such
silence, such order.

ITEM:
Seven stones in a circle make
eight shapes.

ITEM:
Not being birds, we seek our own
windpatterns, fashion
the lute, discover language.

ITEM:
Following the taut strands
that span flower and drainspout,
down the long loops, moving
through the spider's whole house,
we come round to the center
and the patient jewel in its own setting.

Song

By what wild geese were you spawned
that the birds come up to your hand?
I hear them circle and hover,
afraid to fly down here.
Don't they know how well I sweep
my yard? Hair tied back, I leave
my shoes and go out to listen.
They could come downwind
to my house—jaybirds, snowbirds—wing
their wild dance in and out of pine
trees and twist the gray worms down
their bright tongues.

The seeds are scattered, the suet
hangs in the birch tree. Each night
the tree frogs sing to my window:
     brekkit   *brekkit*

For S.,

this girl who is
twisting her lovely face to tell me—
something, her body is
rigid with
language, under her pink blouse
her shoulders
stiffen, her left
hand jerks out a
rhythm to sing by,
the vowels clog in her throat, the
improbable consonants won't
come, she
pauses,
a phrase,
a sentence a whole thought
tumble out on their own,
she tries to catch that tide of language,
then hangs
on one
word, she
labors
for speech,
past inadequate body,
past the rural scene
of the window, past the beasts
busy with lunch, the flowers tied
to the field, each a separate
cup of juices, and the stones
with their mouths sewn shut.

II

Farm Wife

Dark as the spring river, the earth
opens each damp row as the farmer
swings the far side of the field.
The blackbirds flash their red
wing patches and wheel in his wake,
down to the black dirt; the windmill
grinds in its chain rig and tower.

In the kitchen, his wife is baking.
She stands in the door in her long white
gloves of flour. She cocks her head and
tries to remember, turns like the moon
toward the sea-black field. Her belly
is rising, her apron fills like a sail.
She is gliding now, the windmill churns
beneath her, she passes the farmer,
the fine map of the furrows.
The neighbors point to the bone-white
spot in the sky.
                    Let her float
like a fat gull that swoops and circles,
before her husband comes in for supper,
before her children grow up and leave her,
before the pulley cranks her down
the dark shaft, and the church blesses
her stone bed, and the earth seals
its black mouth like a scar.

"The Wife Takes a Child"

She has come next door to practice our piano.
Fat worms, her fingers hover over the keys,
dolce, dolce, advance to a black note.
I call out answers; she blinks a trusting eye.
From the window I can see the phlox
bank and flower, the violets' broad train
at the yard's edge, and beyond, the bee-boxes,
each one baited for summer with a queen.

Love, how long must we reproduce ourselves
in the neighbors' children, bees in false hives,
bright inviting blossoms, mine for a season.
Against the C-scale's awkward lullabye
I carry the offense of my flat belly,
the silent red loss of monthly bleeding.

The Handmaiden

Robert Bryant, 1878–1958,
Rose Peters Bryant, 1877–1914,
Sara Bolling Bryant, 1890–

Five births in eight years, the last
with its terrible flux and no help for it,
their mother was dead, his real wife was dead.
The children parceled out to relatives,
he fed on his sorrow, that hard red berry—
four years, until duty recalled them
and drove his famous temper underground.

After careful interview, she was installed;
gave little, was given little;
prepared the biscuit; instructed
the children by his strict example;
watched them flutter from the house like kites;
stood by as he reeled them back in
on memory's long string.
                              At his death,
his will supplanted all imagination.
What did it matter, to have survived him?
Daily she ties on her bonnet, walks
the half mile to rake, mow or mulch
his family plot. There the two bodies
nestle together under the common stone:
Robert on the left, her own lot to the right,
And at the center his grief-perfected Rose.

Gathering

When the folds of the curtain drew apart, you were sitting in the third row with her, she was slim and beautiful, her mouth was a ripe, purple berry, above the elegant nose her eyes were two roaches, she *wasn't* beautiful, her breasts were cones under the black crepe, she had no hips at all, her hair stroked your cheek like a web. I ran from the stage and drove through rain on the five-lane highway. Behind the barricade the van waited like an oven, the doors were folded back and slick with rain. They were bringing in the bodies from the sea, each one wrapped in burlap. Long, slender cigars, how easily they slid into that open mouth.

•

It was a party. It was a reunion of old friends. It was out on the lawn behind a beautiful house. The shrubbery was old and expensive, the house in need of repair. Beside the stone fence, a cast-iron pot held the dinner. Everyone laughed and chatted. The women in sharkskin dresses displayed triangular swatches of tan. I was lying in the living room. I was not allowed in the sun. I was lying on the antique horsehair sofa, in need of repair. Someone said My God she sunburned in the shade. Everyone laughed. Someone said After all she's twelve months pregnant. Everyone laughed. I noticed the hem had come out of my dress. I noticed my bedroom slippers. I noticed my red legs against the expensive sofa. The young Greek came up and took my hand. After all she's twelve months pregnant, he said. No one said a word. The cook, in a clean apron, brought hot water in the pot, which was old and in need of repair. Outside, the ice, like laughter, was lethal against the expensive crystal.

•

I made no move to stop it. I did nothing but watch. I was standing at the top of the stairs and suddenly my arms were weak, the baby started to roll, away from me, out toward the vertical space above the staggered brown key-board, she was water, graceful, unhurried, she was moving away from me, down across the elbows, along the limp forearms, the ball bearings of the wrists pushed her forward, over the thumbmound, the headline and heartline, she polished my gold ring with her rolling, heading toward the fingers' offering gesture. But slowly the hand closed like a dried leaf, the palm was curling, the thumb moved up to a pinch, and hooked at last the last end of the small, flowered, flannel nightgown.

Birthday Sestina

A crowded nursery, your shelf holds eighteen
photographs, grandchildren and their children,
gray and glossy, each forever a baby.
Across the room, facing down your daughters'
bounty: gazing from a gauzy dream
of Renoir yellows, blues and rose: your picture

over the bedstead. You brought the gilt-edged picture
and bone china to your groom's house—eighteen
months in Penhook, Va., you bawled like a baby.
He was the sixth of eight industrious children;
good stock, but not the chevalier you were dreaming
of. Queen of the Piedmont, the spoiled daughter

of your father's house, oh you were beauty's daughter
with a starched waist and high-swept hair! At eighteen,
before he wooed and wed you, could you picture
him by the wagon, you holding the baby?
The growing yield, a wagonload of children?
How he harvested, year on year, his dreamy

seed's worth! Married to routine, you dreamed
of your father, cried out with fever. In 1918
Papa almost lost you and the baby
you carried. The croup kettle steamed your picture
from its frame. My mother, your oldest daughter,
hid in the closet like a shoe. Children

were dying everywhere. You fed your children
whiskey and sugar, embraced the milky dream
of vapor, nursing the flu like another daughter.
But frailty failed you, gave way to health and eighteen
times remembering as the mantel's picture
gallery flourished and fattened, one baby

after another. Mothers now, we baby
you like the last rose, surround you with children.
Composed beneath your pastel, brass-edged picture,
you choose the veil of cataracts. In the dream
he calls with a soft voice, *Daughter, Daughter,*
and you are beautiful, high-minded, and eighteen.

Claiming Kin

Insistent as a whistle, her voice up
the stairs pried open the blanket's
tight lid and piped me
down to the pressure cooker's steam and rattle.
In my mother's kitchen, the hot iron spit
on signal, the vacuum cleaner whined
and snuffled. Bright face
and a snazzy apron, clicking her long spoons,
how she commandeered the razzle-dazzle!

In the front room I dabbed
the company chairs with a sullen rag.
Pale lump blinking at the light,
I could hear her sing in her shiny kingdom,
the sound drifted out like a bottled message.
It was the voice of a young girl,
who stopped to gather cool moss,
forgetting the errand, spilling the cornmeal,
and cried and cried in her bearish papa's ear.

At night, while I flopped like a fish
on grandma's spool bed, up from her bed
and my wheezing father she rose to the holly,
flat-leaf and Virginia creeper.
Soft ghost, plush as a pillow,
she wove and fruited against the black hours:
red berries and running cedar, green signatures
on the table, on the mantel.

Mother, this poem is from your middle
child who, like your private second self
rising at night to wander the dark house,
grew in the shady places:
a green plant in a brass pot,
rootbound, without blossoms.

Sister

1

Mother's illness pulled you
home on the first bus, me in your wake.
Day and night you illuminate her room
sponging distress from that body,
commanding plants into blossom.
Now, between shifts, we sit like friends
in the kitchen, sharing coffee.

In my favorite snapshot you lean
from your tricycle, arms encircling me—
moon-faced, myopic, immobile
in my blue snowsuit—as if by sheer will
you could lift me on. Who can deny
the gravity of that embrace?
Displaced from my life,
once more angling for this family,
I glide into orbit.

Is it your power to hurt them
I am jealous of?

2

In the recurring dream I am six or seven.
We live in the little house with its yardful of oak,
that treasure of brown hands I raked and piled.

Yes, say my parents, we have the child you need:
they have come for me, two men in suits, carrying machetes.
Outside, under the oaks, the crowd awaits the ceremony.
I've made a perfect likeness—
Same pie face, limp hair, same muslin feedsack gown,
like yours, except the ribbon at the neck is blue.
But when they draw the knives and hack off my head,
rags, string, sawdust, everything pours out but blood
and they know, they will not forgive.
Then we are in the car, driving to Danville,
Mother and Daddy are in the back with me.
As we cross the Banister River Bridge I look down;
my hand sweats on the handle:
leap out and fall to that red sash,
or stay in the car, sweeping toward the blade—

3

O the houses we inhabited—
saplings in a rough square,
a mossy patch, a circle drawn in dirt
and you settled us in.
How to resist the old cookstove,
bright as a tooth in the deep woods?
The nest sat on the rack, a big gray cake,
and when you opened the oven
out of it issued the hornets
with their instinctive venom,

streaming from that stiff breast,
and you went flying down the path,
screaming for Momma, dragging
home your long lethal tail.

•

You midpoint on the stairs, flush with argument;
my father below, rising from his cushion;

you scuttling up and out of reach;
my father settling back with the last word;

visible knees, reproach flung down to the chair,
my father rises with his rolled newspaper,

scuffle of feet, heavy footsteps following—
door slams, locks.

•

You with your tall slender body,
your beaux on the stoop, your local husband,
you with the easy charm you learned from your mother,
you with your talent for children, your perfect loaves,
your sewing machine, that cabinet of bees,
your fierce scissors laboring over cloth and hair
to wreak my transformation.

•

You,
pulling me home in the wagon,
breakneck with your bleating cargo,
until I put out my foot to slow us
and the secret piece of tin
sliced it like a tomato.

•

When we were little
I used to wish you dead;
then hold my breath and sweat
to hear yours
release, intake, relax into sleep.

4

We were playing on the grassy hill
on the long side of the house—a clot
of cousins, all of them boys, all older,
a noisy cluster rearranging its cells,
when the upstairs left window split
its voile curtains and my aunt
leaned out into summer to holler
down at us, calling *me*, holding
out of the window like a flag,

like a dead bird, the britches I'd peed in
and hidden under Grandma Sally's bed.
The rest is the story I was raised on:
how I crouched around back, washing
them out, while you sat on a slab
of rock by the spigot and cried.

5

Anyone else, you would have died. Toxic
in the womb, weighing in early at less
than five pounds, all of it nerve and reckless
appetite, you couldn't even stomach
Mother's milk. Not just the usual colic
and croup for you; brandishing your flair
for the acute, you'd sniff out whatever
disease or disaster was lurking in the district.

Your fourth year was charted like a fever.
With my routine appearance, what could she do
but leave me penned to endlessly reassemble
the coffeepot? As she sponged you by the hour
you thrashed the bed, your eyes swam back in your skull
and you nearly bit your purple tongue in two.

6

A neighbor called for equipment:
whatever embers from the hearth
lay dormant in the basket I'd
tossed into the shed,
fed on the gas-soaked floor
and the shed caught in the wind,
sprouted a great orange growth
that spread to the left
where the feeder calves were penned,
to the right and the dog lots,
bridged to the fence on sumac
where it ran that plank border
eating creosote, ringing
the yard, the house, all of us
at lunch in the kitchen,
with such symmetry:
the family
the circle of fire

The Hen

The neck lodged under a stick,
the stick under her foot,
she held the full white breast
with both hands, yanked up and out,
and the head was delivered of the body.
Brain stuck like a lens; the profile
fringed with red feathers.
Deposed, abstracted,
the head lay on the ground like a coin.
But the rest, released into the yard,
language and direction wrung from it,
flapped the insufficient wings
and staggered forward, convulsed, instinctive—
I thought it was sobbing to see it hump the dust,
pulsing out those muddy juices,
as if something, deep in the gizzard,
in the sack of soft nuggets,
drove it toward the amputated member.
Even then, watching it litter the ground
with snowy refusals, I knew it was this
that held life, gave life,
and not the head with its hard contemplative eye.

The Feast of the Assumption of the Virgin

Matins

Felix rapina. The flap
and whistle of the angel's
wings, the public birth,
the chastened motherhood.
When they led her from her son's
cruel scaffolding, she wanted
no more miracles. Now this.
Plucked up to heaven, a pressed
flower—her body is used
for a million statuary.

Nones

The church sweats in its dark stone.
The triptych, a pamphlet of roses,
flanks the altar. In one stained
panel of window, Joseph provides detail.
The Madonna mourns from a nearby table;
one hand is raised
as if reaching for fruit. Among
the murmuring candles, a solicitor
spews his secret into her ear.

Compline

Mary,
Holy Vessel, Queen of the Martyrs:
in the mountains of Zakopane

the rutted street swells
with women, bringing you flowers.
See how they cradle

the passionate blossoms. Precious
Mother, the village is blooming. Here,
in a row by the plain wood houses,

here, by the roadside,
the young girls are gathered.
Each wears white lace, hand-made

for marriage; each
is chosen, blessed by the father;
and when the bells release

a shower of pollen,
each mouth opens to rapture
like a wound.

III

Damage

It didn't suckle. That
was the first indication.

Looking back, I know how much I knew.
The repetitious bloodfall,

the grating at the door of bone,
the afterbirth stuck in my womb like a scab.

Others were lucky,
response was taken from them.

Each time I bathe him
in his little tub, I think

How easy to let go

Let go

House

This orphaned house. Its needs, its presences.

Something brought us here—how else
could we, raw mourners,
have found it
tucked under the hill beside the sea?

Everything still stands
from previous lives: well, woodstove,
the feather tick imprinted
with so many bodies.

This place survives their multiple
amputations. The tug on the nipple
after the baby is gone,
after the breast is gone.

Trimming the wicks, setting the oak table—
when I move the air gives,
feels polished, I fill
the waiting sleeve with movement.

And everywhere the proprietary swallows.

•

The body learns to incorporate its pain.
Sorrow lodged in the kitchen.
Stepsister. She-who-remembers. There,

in the corner, she worked her practical
arts—intaglio and salt-cure:

>A splash of brine on the table,
>hot iron, knife-slip, a scar,
>a trough, the table webs
>with stains and scratches.

>Deep into the water's
>grain, a boat engraves
>its habits. The wake
>has healed but retains
>the shape of the hull,
>the wound of the rudder.

•

I have my routine.

The garden calls me to its harvesting.
The well needs me to draw up water.

From the seawind, I read tomorrow's
weather. The swallows surround us.

Evenings, we sit inside,
under the wing of the unfinished attic.

Here, in this place, this parentage,
we live with loss, a child's repeating absence.

The Letter

She sits at the table
with her small collection of treasure.
Chooses from it a shell whose delicate edges whorl
inward to a palm, a lifeprint.
Inside this pastel saucer,
parsley and chives recall a Japanese garden:
clean, immutable.
If only she were there,
a single tiny figure by the pool,
holding the letter.
If only she were rock, tree, clear water.

April, 1945

Soft *chink*—
a dog stretching its chain in sleep,
but he has no dog. Beside him,
his wife's nasal exhalation.
Cinched his pajamas. Plucked
the gun, erect, from the corner.
Stalked the dark house, along
the striped oak toward linoleum.
Sprawling there, saw her nightgown
filling the bedroom doorway as if
on the washline, bright with sun,
supple, inhaling, gathering light
and wind to its center, its bosom,
that wet red sponge.

The Waning Moon

Couched in pillows, coaching him
toward her open blouse and its ripe
nipple, feeling the bite, the shudder,
thinking

                    This is mine

she always wanted children—boys
with soft purses between their legs,
girls to call help or Mama, the purple
bundle to crack from her thighs,
a lump inside her

                    Here is the skull
                    here the foot split from a fin

And before, her body grown useful,
the salty waters gathering. And loss:
month after month, the seed
hosed from its hammock.

At night, she sifts the dried
dillweed, worries the bread dough
into a long loaf. And when her husband
rolls toward her in the brass bed,
she chooses chastity.

Executioner

You were a man with only your own resources,
nothing to stand on, no rope, no rafters.
Alone in your cell,
you tied your belt to the grill
of the window and leaned into death,
such labor that never relinquished
until your lungs folded like tissue,
until your temples were brought to blossom
and the heart, in its conviction, overcome.

The Victim

Who could remember cause? Both
sought injury, and God knows
they were perfectly matched for pain.
Fenced into their landscape of passion,
each moved to the center and set upon
the other. Always, she would deploy
the tease, the jab, the deft tongue,
until his arm swung out on its hinge,
coming flat-handed against her face,
recoiled, then stiffened to thrust
his fist into her open mouth.
This was not the only violation.
When a child is struck by her father,
she crawls toward him, not away,
bound by habits not yet broken.

The Burial

Vermont, 1889

March, when the ground softened
and the men could dig the multiple graves,
was time enough to examine the winter's losses.
But the girl from Lower Cabot—
when they opened the coffins
to match the dead to their markers,
they found the corpse in terrific disarray:
bodice torn from the throat,
face sealed in distortion, eyes
open, the coins nowhere in evidence,
and in each fist a wad of her own dark hair.

The Marriage

Under its angry skin, her grief
ripens: succulent, wound-color.
She knew there were other women—
his baroque excuses for silence—
but knew in the weaker hemisphere
of her heart, that stringent
muscle pumping in, valved open.
Hinged clam, living for fifteen years
on grit and gravel, housed now against
the weather, she has the car, the kids,
an appetite for garbage. He's got
a new wife, wants her to take him in,
produce a pearl.

The Birth

The first would be five now.
She remembers herself in family photos,
dark hair braided and bandaged.
She had to work
at the second, Scorpio,
who skulks through her dreams
distempered and bony. But this one—
full-term, sharp-chinned, surfacing
face up—needs no such conjuring. She says,
"This is your son," fingering
the rosary of his spine. You scan
her pouchy belly. You study the phonebook.
You pocket your great thumbs.
You step off the distance of the room.
Applying the active mouth like a leech,
she feels the persuasive bloodbeat,
unfurls the fist, the palm
already mapped and pencilled in.

The Drowned Man

How I love you in your hopeless act.
The black wound on the skin of the pond;
the small body already stiffening:
and so you entered that dark closet of water.

But your wife on the shore
turned away from the lost child,
chose the two live children rooted behind her
receiving the permanent visions of their sleep,
chose life,
chose to live with ice at the heart.

Harvest

The farmer circles the pasture
checking fences. Deep
in the broomstraw, the dove withholds

her three notes. The sky
to the southwest is uniformly
blue. Years of plowing under

have brought this red clay to its
green conclusion.
Down back,

the herd
clusters to the loading pen.
Only disease or dogpack

could alter such order. Is that
what he asks for in the late
fields, the falling afternoon?

The Quickening

All evening she shifts through the house,
gathering purpose.
Everything is changed now,
she has money in her purse,
she has a weapon.
The moon, snagged in the oak,
is rising out of its black hand,
lights the bedroom.
Under that grim eye,
the bed is luminous, refractive.
As he steps incautiously into its white field,
she will be waiting, approximating sleep:
Like the baby suspended inside her.
Like a hawk adrift in its fine solution of clouds.

The Visit

The afternoon spreads its fingers on the lawn,
and such light as penetrates the shrubs
enters the house with hesitation.
I have come from a great distance
to find my father asleep in his large brown chair.
Why isn't he out in the fields, our common passion?
I want to wake him with kisses,
I want to reach out and stroke his hand.
But I turn away, without speech or gesture,
having for so long withheld my body from him.

All Souls' Day

Confronting frost,
the trees assume their attitudes of pain.
Who can think of the ocean?
its permanent surf, its violated sand.

She takes off her glasses,
folds them into their tapestry
envelope. After coffee,
after she straightens the kitchen,
after her TV program,
she is going to pray for the children.

Scarved and suited for autumn,
she will stand, as in the park,
where they are gathered, that each
may sail his little sin into temperate waters.

THE FORCES OF PLENTY

(1983)

In memory of my parents
Lloyd G. Bryant
Zue Y. Bryant

I

The Spire

In the Bavarian steeple, on the hour,
two figures emerge from their scalloped house
carrying sledges that they clap, in turn,
against the surface of the bell. By legend
they are summer and winter, youth and age,
as though the forces of plenty and of loss
played equally on the human soul, extracted
easily the same low bronze note spreading
upward from the encumbrance of the village,
past alluvial fields to the pocked highland
where cattle shift their massive heads
at this dissonance, this faint redundant
pressure in the ears, in the air.

From the village, the mountain seems
a single stone, a single blank completion.
Seeing the summit pierce the abstract heavens,
we reconstruct the valley on the mountain—
a shepherd propped against his crook, birds
enthralled on a branch, the branch feathering
the edge of the canvas—transposing
such forms as can extend the flawed earth
and embody us, intact, unaltering, among
the soft surprising trees of childhood,
mimosa, honey locust and willow.

Wood in the midst of woods, the village
houses are allied in a formal shape
beside a stream, the streets concluding

at the monument. Again the ravishing moment
of the bell: the townspeople, curious
or accustomed, stop to count the strokes,
odd or even—the confectioner counting out
the lavender candies for his customer,
the butcher, the greengrocer, the surgeon
and the constable—as the housewife
stands on the stoop, shaking her mop,
and sees the dust briefly veil the air,
an algebra of swirling particles.

A Fugue

The body, a resonant bowl:
the irreducible gist of wood,
that memorized the turns
of increase and relinquishing:
the held silence
where formal music will be quarried
by the cry of the strings,
the cry of the mind,
under the rosined bow.

The deaf listen
with compensatory hands,
touching the instrument.
Musicians also
listen, and speak, with their hands.

Such elemental implements.
The eye trains on a grid of ink,
and the fingers quicken,
habitual, learnéd,
to recover the arterial melody.

3

The long habit of living
indisposes us to dying.
In this measured space,
a drastic weeping.

•

Music depends
on its own diminishing.
Like the remembered dead,
roused from silence
and duplicated, the song heard
is sound leaving the ear.

•

Medicine too is a temporal art.
Each day, children
are rendered into your keeping.
And so you take up your instruments
to make whole, to make live,
what others made.

4

Pure science:
the cello in your lap;
the firm misleading bodies
of your own children
in your brother's room.
His illness is adult, and lethal.
You place the bow
and Beethoven turns again
from the stern physician
to annotate the page:
cantabile—

          meaning
not birdsong, windsong,
wind in the flue, bell, branch,
but the human voice,
distinct and perishable.

And you play for him.

Jug Brook

Beyond the stone wall,
the deer should be emerging from their yard.
Lank, exhausted, they scrape at the ground
where roots and bulbs will send forth
new definitions. The creek swells in its ditch;
the field puts on a green glove.
Deep in the woods, the dead ripen,
and the lesser creatures turn to their commission.

Why grieve for the lost deer,
for the fish that clutter the brook,
the kingdoms of midge that cloud its surface,
the flocks of birds that come to feed.
The earth does not grieve.
It rushes toward the season of waste—

On the porch the weather shifts,
the cat dispatches
another expendable animal from the field.
Soon she will go inside to cull her litter,
addressing each with a diagnostic tongue.
Have I learned nothing? God,
into whose deep pocket our cries are swept,
it is you I look for
in the slate face of the water.

The Medium

My father struck me when I first told
what I had witnessed;
my mother plucked her beaded chain.
But no matter how I scrubbed my left hand,
the lines, like trenches, emptied into the palm.

Sixty years with these companions
who rise from exile
to pour their diminishing cupfuls into me.
Sometimes, it's only a breath swollen with fog.
Or a column of light on the stairs, by the cupboard,
displacing the air and its busy dust motes.
But when I hear their pitiful signals of grief. . . .

•

The white field has risen over the fenceline.
I sit for hours by the window,
like any old woman.

On the west side of the house,
a drift flutters gracefully against the clapboards,
like the dress she wore to greet her lover
the night his knife dazzled into her body.

This is the Crown of Winter,
the last storm that can raise the level of snow.
Soon the sun will begin its hot subtraction.

•

A small square moon:
the neighbor's light in the distance.
Imagine,
her husband hunched over supper,
a child nested in her lap.
How could I have a life?
I was their tether,
the incompleted dead, the stubborn ones,

who will not forestall my own soul's slow erasure.
After my bones are put on their shelf
there will come the usual solstice,
not pain but the absence of pain,
terrible, unwarranted.
And then the second death:

a stranger will sleep in this bed without dreams;
will wrap himself against the evening's chill;
will credit the wind with my whispers;
will straighten the portrait again and again
without revelation;
hearing nothing, believing nothing.

The Gymnast

I have beaten the blank mat, but the name
that tolls from the wide throat of the crowd
is *Nadia, Nadia.*
Magic is not earned and is not fair.
After repeated labor against
the body's meat and strict bone, still
with each leap or press or stretch or somersault,
my flesh in its new attitude
mourns like a lover for the ground. And Nadia
balances on the dust beside the beam,
she takes the shapes of a leaf in slow wind.

Others climb after that mark;
I will settle
for the long hours of practice at her side,
my error reconciled in her correction—
mother and sister, midwife, teacher,
I am earth, earth, from which her body leapt into the air.

Pastoral

Crouched in the yard,
he brings his dirty hands up to his mouth.
No, No, I say. *Yuck. Hurt.*

These are sounds he will recognize.
I say them when he takes an orange
with its hidden seeds and allergenic juice.
No. Yuck. Bad orange. Or reaming
from his mouth a wad of bread,
a lump of odorous cheese.
The fire will hurt.
The stick will break and stab you
in the heart. The reckless wheel,
the cool suggestive music of the pond.

Overhead, summer spreads its blue scarf;
a light wind bends the hollyhocks;
birds, trees—
everything the way I might have dreamed it,
he stands in the grass,
weighing a handful of berries,
a handful of stones.

The Spring

Beneath the fabric of leaves,
sycamore, beech, black oak,
in the slow residual movement
of the pool;
           in the current
braiding over the wedged branch,
and pouring from the ledge,
urgent, lyric,
           the source
marshalls every motion
to the geometric plunder of rock—
arranging a socket of water,
a cold estate
where the muscle wound
in the deep remission of light
waits
      for the white enamel dipper,
the last release, the rush,
the blunt completion

Why She Says No

Two friends at the close of summer.
On the path, the birds quicken.
While he talks,
he strokes her arm in one direction
as if it had a nap of feathers.
How handsomely the heart's valves
lie open for the blood rush.
How her body also begins to open.
At the edge of the woods, they pass
goldenrod and lupin, the tall thin weeds
supple as a whale's teeth
conducting the avid fish to the interior.

She is not the mouth, whatever you think
and even though she craves
this closeness, its rich transfusion.
Desire is the mouth, the manipulating heart,
the wing. Above her,
the branches of the pines, their quilled expanse
blanketing the subtler vegetation.

The Diviner

The danger surfaced in the fontanel.
I held your head on my arm,
whispering lullabies into your sweet hot neck;
by the second week that was forbidden.
Then you swam alone
on your white sheet. Robed, masked,
I put my face as close as I could get it
to see what the sickness pulsed and signaled.

.

When I was little,
my father used to light a Lucky
and blow warm smoke, like a secret,
into my sore ear. I was amazed
it never escaped through the other ear,
nor any orifice Mother peered into—
to be housing the breath of my father!

.

Now you are growing and closing
everywhere against me.
The melded hemispheres of bone
have sealed my small window
as I pace the dry ground with my wand,
trying to hold the stick without bias,
trying to learn what the surface will not tell,
until the green wood plunges, nearly twists

from my grip: there's water here—
but how much? and how deep?

Alba

My daughter calls me into light to see
the world has altered while she slept.
Like my mother's voice that pulled me
from the clarifying dark, her voice
will not relent, a bell at my ear
rehearsing gladly for her own child
in whom my long thirst for sleep
will reappear.
                Hush. Hush.
My work there is not finished.
Before morning overwhelms the house,
I must ford the tall grasses—
Then the circle of birches,
the stranger's face not yet in full shadow.

II

For My Husband

Is it a dream,
the way we huddle over the board,
our fingers touching on the slick button?
The Ouija stammers under so much doubt,
finally reaches L, then O,
pauses under its lettered heaven,
and as it veers toward *loss* and the long past
that lodges with us, you press toward *love*,
and the disk stalls
               outside
a cry is loosed from the bay,
but you are looking for two swans
on a glass lake, a decade of roses—
oh my lonely, my precious loaf,
can't we say out loud the parent word,
longing,
          whose sad head
looms over any choice you make?

A Marriage Poem

1

Morning: the caged baby
sustains his fragile sleep.
The house is a husk against weather.
Nothing stirs—inside, outside.
With the leaves fallen,
the tree makes a web on the window
and through it the world
lacks color or texture,
like stones in the pasture
seen from this distance.

This is what is done with pain:
ice on the wound,
the isolating tourniquet—
as though to check an open vein
where the self pumps out of the self
would stop the second movement of the heart,
diastolic, inclusive:
to love is to siphon loss into that chamber.

2

What does it mean when a woman says,
"my husband,"
if she sits all day in the tub;
if she worries her life like a dog a rat;
if her husband seems familiar but abstract,
a bandaged hand she's forgotten how to use.

They've reached the middle years.
Spared grief, they are given dread
as they tend the frail on either side of them.
Even their marriage is another child,
grown rude and querulous
since death practiced on them and withdrew.

He asks of her only a little lie,
a pale copy drawn from the inked stone
where they loll beside the unicorn,
great lovers then, two strangers
joined by appetite:
                          it frightens her,
to live by memory's poor diminished light.
She wants something crisp and permanent,
like coral—a crown, a trellis,
an iron shawl across the bed
where they are laced together,
the moon bleaching the house,
their bodies abandoned—

3

In last week's mail,
still spread on the kitchen table,
the list of endangered species.
How plain the animals are,
quaint, domestic,
but the names lift from the page:
Woundfin. Whooping Crane. Squawfish.
Black-footed Ferret. California Least Tern.

Dearest, the beast of Loch Ness, that shy,
broad-backed, two-headed creature,
may be a pair of whales or manatee,
male and female,
driven from their deep mud nest,
who cling to each other,
circling the surface of the lake.

Exile

The widow refuses sleep, for sleep pretends
that it can bring him back.
In this way,
the will is set against the appetite.
Even the empty hand moves to the mouth.
Apart from you,
I turn a corner in the city and find,
for a moment, the old climate,
the little blue flower everywhere.

Blue Ridge

Up there on the mountain road, the fireworks
blistered and subsided, for once at eye level:
spatter of light like water flicked from the fingers;
the brief emergent pattern; and after the afterimage bled
from the night sky, a delayed and muffled thud
that must have seemed enormous down below,
the sound concomitant with the arranged
threat of fire above the bleachers.
I stood as tall and straight as possible,
trying to compensate, trying not to lean in my friend's
direction. Beside me, correcting height, he slouched
his shoulders, knees locked, one leg stuck out
to form a defensive angle with the other.
Thus we were most approximate
and most removed.
                              In the long pauses
between explosions, he'd signal conversation
by nodding vaguely toward the ragged pines.
I said my children would have loved the show.
He said we were watching youth at a great distance,
and I thought how the young
are truly boring, unvaried as they are
by the deep scar of doubt, the constant afterimage
of regret—no major tension in their bodies, no tender
hesitation, they don't yet know
that this is so much work, scraping
from the self its multiple desires; don't yet know
fatigue with self, the hunger for obliteration
that wakes us in the night at the dead hour

and fuels good sex.

                    Of course I didn't say it.
I realized he watched the fireworks
with the cool attention he had turned on women
dancing in the bar, a blunt uninvested gaze
calibrating every moving part, thighs,
breasts, the muscles of abandon.
I had wanted that gaze on me.
And as the evening dwindled to its nub,
its puddle of tallow, appetite without object,
as the men peeled off to seek
the least encumbered consolation
and the women grew expansive with regard—
how have I managed so long to stand among the paired
bodies, the raw pulsing music driving
loneliness into the air like scent,
and not be seized by longing,
not give anything to be summoned
into the larger soul two souls can make?
Watching the fireworks with my friend,
so little ease between us,
I see that I have armed myself;
fire changes everything it touches.

Perhaps he has foreseen this impediment.
Perhaps when he holds himself within himself,
a sheathed angular figure at my shoulder,
he means to be protective less of him
than me, keeping his complicating rage

inside his body. And what would it solve
if he took one hand from his pocket,
risking touch, risking invitation—
if he took my hand it would not alter
this explicit sadness.
                        The evening stalls,
the fireworks grow boring at this remove.
The traffic prowling the highway at our backs,
the couples, the families scuffling on the bank
must think us strangers to each other. Or,
more likely, with the celebrated fireworks thrusting
their brilliant repeating designs above the ridge,
we simply blur into the foreground,
like the fireflies dragging among the trees
their separate, discontinuous lanterns.

The Couple

"Like a boy," she said,
and opened her robe to show him
the plate of bone and its center flower
of black thread.

                Only flesh, he thought,
the breast cut loose from its net of skin.
And if she could not dote on him,
he'd answer her bell in the bedroom
where she is lodged among the pillows,
her spread hair weightless,

but now he knows how heavy her head is,
how it rolls on her shoulder
when he pulls her off the floor,
how, as they stumble toward the bed,
old woman, old man,
he hears two threading voices—
the one stammering in his chest,
and the one who calls him in the thickening air.

Eurydice

It bears no correlation
to the living world. It is
as if a malice toward all things
malleable, mutable,
had seized the universe
and emptied its spherical alleys.

How could you think it,
that I would choose to stay, or break
under the journey back? Like a dog
I had followed your unraveling
skein of sound—
                Orpheus,
                        standing
between me and iridescent earth,
you turned to verify the hell
I was thrown to, and got
what you needed for your songs.
They do not penetrate the grave,
I cannot hear them, I cannot know
how much you mourn.
                    But I mourn:
against my will
I forgive you over and over,
transfixed by your face
emerging like a moon across your shoulder,
your shocked mouth calling "Wife, wife"
as you let me go.

Epithalamium

The river,
the white boat,
the moon like new money:

This is the union of air and water.

My husband moves easily
among the cluster of friends.
You stand at the rail to watch
the new couple,

until the two of them
leave the dream,
it having become a parable of longing.

•

I go over the side and down the rope ladder
into the muskrat house.
The walls are lined with mute, oriental faces.

I must be there to give instruction,
coming as I do
from my strong marriage,

but it is you who goes straightway
to the large book.
I'm sure it is you—
the characteristic raised knuckle,
the frame hunched with its own weight.

Earth shaping us on all sides,
I put my face against the cool mud wall:
this is our element.

•

Look, Keith:

on the shore
my husband builds me a fire.
The light pools on the sand.
It is this fire, his fire,
that weds us over and over.

Sal gives Elaine his open hand
and we stand in a circle
like four walls, each
of another color,

our shadows cast out
behind us into evening,
as, at the center,
the fire burns recklessly
to give us its definition.

Quarrel

Since morning they have been quarreling—
the sun pouring its implacable white bath
over the birches, each one undressing
slyly, from the top down—and they hammer
at each other with their knives, nail files,
graters of complaint as the day unwinds,
the plush clouds lowering a gray matte
for the red barn. Lunch, the soup
like batting in their mouths, last week,
last year, they're moving on to always
and never, their shrill pitiful children
crowd around but they see the top of this
particular mountain, its glacial headwall,
the pitch is terrific all through dinner,
and they are committed, the sun long gone,
the two of them back to back in the blank
constricting bed, like marbles on aluminum—
O this fierce love
that needs to reproduce in one another
wounds inflicted by the world.

Year's End

The fingers lie in the lap,
separate, lonely, as in the field
the separate blades of grass
shrivel or grow tall.

We sat together in the little room,
the walls blotched with steam,
holding the baby as if the two of us
could breathe for him and were not helpless.
Upstairs, his sister turned in her sleep
as the phone rang—

to have wakened to a child's cry,
gagged and desperate,
and then repeat that terror when the call
split the quiet house and centered
its dire message:
                    a child was dead
and his mother so wrung by grief
she stared and stared
at the moon on its black stalk,
the road glistening like wire.
Rubbing the window clear of steam
as a child rubs sleep from its eyes,
and looking past the fence to where
he had plunged the sled up and down the hill,
we could still see the holes his feet made,
a staggered row of graves
extracting darkness from the snow.

When morning brought the new year in,
the fever broke, and fresh snow
bandaged the tracks on the hill.
For a long time we stayed in the room,
listening to him breathe,
like refugees who listen to the sea,
unable to fully rejoice, or fully grieve.

Liebesgedicht

I love you as my other self, as the other
self of the tree is not the pale tree
in the flat hand of the river, but the earth
that holds, is held by, the root of the tree.
This is how the earth loves the river,
and why its least fold solicits each
impulsive stream until the gathered water
makes of earth a passage to the sea.

I'd like to draw a lesson from this figure,
and find some comfort in the way the larger
world rings with such dependencies.
But if I see ourselves in earth and water,
I also see one taken from the other,
the rivening wind loosed against the tree.

III

January

After days of putting down my poem
to wipe the chair, I see
the skin of the room is oozing pitch.
Steep as a church, a bishop's hat,
the roof is lined with spruce,
and this close to the stove
the heat has opened the sap line
at each dark flaw, as though it tapped
a living tree. Everyday, a pure emanation,
the syrup bleeds to the surface of the wood.

Now, a length of softwood in its craw,
the stove crackles with resin,
and the room itself
stretches and cracks with heat, cold,
the walls' mediation between them.
There are three pale coins of resin
in the usual place on the arm of the chair.
And the momentary flies,
hatched behind the wallboard
or in the pores of the old beams,
stagger down the window's white page.

If I think I am apart from this, I am a fool.
And if I think the black engine of the stove
can raise in me the same luminous waking,
I am still a fool,
since I am the one who keeps the fire.

The Apology

Hurt dogs crawl under a bush.
A hurt friend circles the house,
refusing to look in.
He makes a grave commotion in the yard
and the jay elevates the clamor of *betrayal,*
betrayal, flashing its shiny
edges from the pine.

You call through the glass.
No answer.
He's busy with his curses,
scuffing up a froth of dandelions—
isn't this what you wanted,
your own grievance, that sets the table
with one white plate?
                      Water on stones,
horses dozing upright in their stalls,
the pink of a weak sky—recalling
the tertiary theme of some great work,
you cross the grass, moving toward him
the way one greets an animal,
extending the hand.

Rescue

But if she has eaten the food of the dead,
she cannot wholly return to the upper air.

All morning you squat in the weeds,
your head small and still
like the head of the snake at rest
on a green blade: no terror for you
in his dense body, you would follow him
into the tangle of brush by the barn
to see whatever house he keeps there.

I watch you watching the snake
or gathering the fallen bird,
the dog in the road, those stiff bodies
from whom you cannot withhold your tenderness.
As if they were your children,
they call you again and again into deep water,
as I wait on the dock,
braiding the long line that knots and tangles.

Talking the Fire Out

1

The stanchioned cows behind him,
the assembled odors,
the dwindling closets of hay—

A farmer stands at the door of the barn:
When to plant, when to harvest:

he studies the remedial clouds,
the rehearsed fields,
red, ridged, and the air
palpable with rain.

2

In that latitude, *come look*
might mean the long bellpull
swaying from a rafter of the barn—two snakes
mating, blacksnakes, barn snakes,
a farmer's charm;
               might mean
bring a chair to the field and watch
a kingsnake, wrapped around a moccasin,
squeezing it like a stopped heart,
finally unwind, unhinge its jaws
and swallow the jeweled head,
the rest of it shuddering in all day

until the king sidles down the furrow
with an extra tongue.
                         Nothing is learned
by turning away. Indian summer,
when we harvested the deathweed
or cut and bound the yellow loaves of hay,
the boys brought every species
to the ninth-grade lab—kingsnake,
blacksnake, copperhead, cottonmouth—
and jar after jar of hazardous yield
struck at the glass.

3

My father in the doorway
with his usual semaphore—

why is it always the same gesture
for *hello* and *goodbye*?
He keeps his elbow tucked,
like a cop,
or does he only want to ask a question?

Away from home,
I take it as a blessing,
the vertical forearm,
the seamed, outfacing palm.

4

If you have a call,
you cradle the injured limb
and lean over the burn
as though kneeling,

but do you talk to the flesh,
to provoke its deep revulsion?
or must you sing directly
to the fire, soothing the beast
of the fire, calling it
out of the hand,
                    a poultice of words
drawing off the sultry residue
until the flush recedes,
leaving original flesh,
no blister, no scar.

5

Who can distinguish knowledge
from belief? Against
the dangers in your own house,
you take up every weapon—
                    Listen:

my father killed a copperhead
with a switch. Out fishing,
coming on it by the pond, knowing
the exact angle and trusting it,
he flicked the weed against its back
as he had often cast his lean line
over secretive waters.

6

Nothing is learned by turning away,
nothing surmounted.

Scattering its wise colors everywhere,
over the red barn, the red fields,
the sun is going down,
and due east, parallel on the horizon,
one of its children up-
rising catches the light
in a round bucket,

as I bend to my work,
crooning over the hurt bodies,
muttering on the page.

Daughter

There is one grief worse than any other.

When your small feverish throat clogged, and quit,
I knelt beside the chair on the green rug
and shook you and shook you,
but the only sound was mine shouting you back,
the delicate curls at your temples,
the blue wool blanket,
your face blue,
your jaw clamped against remedy—

how could I put a knife to that white neck?
With you in my lap,
my hands fluttering like flags,
I bend instead over your dead weight
to administer a kiss so urgent, so ruthless,
pumping breath into your still body,
counting out the rhythm for how long until
the second birth, the second cry
oh Jesus that sudden noisy musical inhalation
that leaves me stunned
by your survival.

Letter from Vermont

In San Francisco, spring was not a season
but an interim with rain and a gentle switch
in the wind from the sea. The bay on one side,
the clean city on the other,
we moved in the clutch of friends
down the steep steps—
                        as I pictured you
standing half in, half out of water,
you glossed the houses, history
fixed in each façade, and we received
a découpage of gardens, trees of fuchsia,
the queen's erotic earrings, and gardenias,
again in trees, the aisle among them
redolent and bruised.
                        Does it wear well,
that civil promise camouflaging rock?
The sea gives, the sea takes back,
the waves lick the women's bodies on the beach.
What is *human*, and *moral*, if not,
rising out of winter's vast denial,
this other flowering:
a deep release
such as overtakes the cloistered animals
as the last snow shreds
in the dilating pupil of the lake,
and birds return to the dull sky
their nearly legible music.

The Happiness Poems

A small figure going up the mountain—
not really a mountain, but a cliff,
a fist of rock carved first by the river,
then by the highway, and now patched
with brush and trees. Here and there
a birch among the evergreens,
and the steady red jacket like a flag.
Surely no one could break a trail
straight up, carrying groceries—
but from here at the Amoco
someone climbs through birch and hemlock,
carrying home two large brown bags,
someone takes a shortcut
straight up the side of a mountain.

        •

If there could be jubilation in the world!
The snow-draped south field
numbers four puddles of brown grass,
it's spring, there are healthy children
in the neighborhood, the lilac beginning—

        •

She lost them all,
and she is someone who knows someone I know.
I try to be happy,
warming outside like a shrub,

until the siren duplicates
that cry that stops the blood.
I want to be happy
in my small unsheltered garden,
my husband a stalk in the wind's teeth,
and our two seasonal blossoms,
one Sweet William,
one delicate wood anemone.

The Bat

Reading in bed, full of sentiment
for the mild evening and the children
asleep in the adjacent rooms, hearing them
cry out now and then the brief reports
of sufficient imagination, and listening
at the same time compassionately
to the scrabble of claws, the fast treble
in the chimney—
                          then it was out,
not a trapped bird
beating at the seams of the ceiling,
but a bat lifting toward us, falling away.

Dominion over every living thing,
large brain, a choice of weapons—
Shuddering, in the lit hall
we swung repeatedly against
its rising secular face
until it fell; then
shoveled it into the yard for the cat,
who shuttles easily between two worlds.

Sweet Everlasting

Swarming over the damp ground with pocket lenses
that discover and distort like an insect's
compound eye, the second grade
slows, stops at the barrier on the path.
They straddle the horizontal trunk, down for months;
rub the rough track of the saw, then focus
on the new shoots at the other end—
residual, suggestive.
I follow the children into open land
above the orchard, its small clouds tethered
to the grass, where we gather
samples of the plentiful white bud
that stipples the high pasture, and name it
by the book: wooly stem, pale lanceolate leaves;
the one called Everlasting. The punishment for doubt
is doubt—my father's death has taught me that.
Last week, he surfaced in a dream as promised,
as, at night, the logic of earth subsides
and stars appear to substantiate
what we could not see. But when I woke,
I remembered nothing that could tell me
which among those distant pulsing inconclusive signs
were active, which extinguished—
remembered, that is,
nothing that could save him.

For My Mother

When does the soul leave the body?
Since early morning you have not moved—
only your head moves, thrown back
with each deliberate breath,
the one sound that matters in the room.
My brother is here, my sister,
two of your sisters, ripples
widening from the bed.
The nurses check and measure,
keeping the many records.
Are you afraid?
Are you dreaming of what is past, lost,
or is this sleep some other preparation?
My sister has put your rings
on my finger; it seems like your hand
stroking the white brow,
unable to release you,
not even after you have asked for death—

And we know nothing about such pain,
except that it has weaned you from us,
and from the reedy, rusted
sunflowers outside the window,
drooping over the snow like tongueless bells.

For My Father

1. ELEGY

Turning from a loss,
as if turning from an open window,
its local composition:
limbs juxtaposed against the sky,
juncture of sky and hillock,
the stark debrided tree.

Autumn, and the shucked leaves
are eating *green,* absorbing it
even as they are severed or detaching—
red is what red leaves repel. Any abstraction
names a consequence.

He is not here
He is not here

Halfway through a life, seeing leaves
the color of fire and of wounds
swaddle the base of the broad
deciduous tree,
you turn from the window's

slice of terrible radiance
to face the cluttered interior on which it falls.

2. PITTSYLVANIA COUNTY

In the front yard, my father and his son
are playing ball, the round egg arcs
toward a lap of brown leather, the sound
of an ax on green wood, a bass
hitting the water. The boy
could do this forever—only one glove
between them and he has it—the fireflies
already discernible on the hillside,
the grass wet, he doesn't falter
as he skirts the waist-high crabapple tree
or backs across the graveled drive.
What am I after? Not shagging flies
on the lawn with my father, and not
drying the last dish with a fresh towel.
My father is a stationary target
through increasing dark, and out from my brother's
cocked proficient arm, the ball leaps,
of its own volition, into his hand.

3. NEW ENGLAND GRAVEYARD

It is a foreign symmetry, unlike anything
in the earth's surface rubble—
the headstones grouped by family
to organize the sacred rows; the flowers
at the fresh site
forced blooms with exposed
glands of pollen and the widest throats;
even the neat packages
of food, each container marked
with the names of the living.
If there is a life beyond the body,
I think we have no use for order
but are buoyed past our individuating fear,
and that memory is not,
as now, a footprint filling with water.

THE LOTUS FLOWERS

(1987)

For Fran, and for Louise

Man is in love and loves what vanishes.

—W. B. YEATS

I

The Last Class

Put this in your notebooks:
All verse is occasional verse.
In March, trying to get home, distracted
and impatient at Gate 5 in the Greyhound station,
I saw a drunk man bothering a woman.
A poem depends on its detail
but the woman had her back to me,
and the man was just another drunk,
black in this case, familiar, dirty.
I moved past them both, got on the bus.

There is no further action to report.
The man is not a symbol. If what he said to her
touches us, we are touched by a narrative
we supply. What he said was, "I'm sorry,
I'm sorry," over and over, "I'm sorry,"
but you must understand he frightened the woman,
he meant to rob her of those few quiet
solitary moments sitting down,
waiting for the bus, before she headed home
and probably got supper for her family,
perhaps in a room in Framingham,
perhaps her child was sick.

My bus pulled out, made its usual turns
and parted the formal gardens from the Common,
both of them camouflaged by snow.
And as it threaded its way to open road,
leaving the city, leaving our sullen classroom,

I postponed my satchel of your poems
and wondered who I am to teach the young,
having come so far from honest love of the world;
I tried to recall how it felt
to live without grief; and then I wrote down
a few tentative lines about the drunk,
because of an old compulsion to record,
or sudden resolve not to be self-absorbed
and full of dread—
                    I wanted to salvage
something from my life, to fix
some truth beyond all change, the way
photographers of war, miles from the front,
lift print after print into the light,
each one further cropped and amplified,
pruning whatever baffles or obscures,
until the small figures are restored
as young men sleeping.

Visiting the Graves

All day we travel from bed to bed, our children
clutching homemade bouquets of tulips and jonquils,
hyacinth, handfuls of yellow salad from the fields.
In Pittsylvania County, our dead face east,
my great-grandfather and his sons facing
what is now a stranger's farm. And here
is my father, under the big oak, near the stone
we watched him weep beside for twenty years,
and my mother beside him, the greenest slab of grass.
By horse, it was hours to Franklin County,
to Liberty Christian Church where her mother lies—
the children squabble in the car, roll on the velvet
slope of the churchyard, pout or laugh as we point out
the gap in the mountain where *her* mother's grave
is underwater, the lake lapping the house, the house
still standing like a tooth. We tell them how
we picked huckleberries from the yard,
tell them what a huckleberry is, but the oldest
can't keep straight who's still alive, the smallest
wants her flowers back—who can blame them,
this far from home, tired of trying
to climb a tree of bones. They fall asleep
halfway down the road, and we fall silent too,
who were taught to remember and return,
my sister is driving, I'm in the back,
the sky before us a broken field of cloud.

Feast Day

If you wanted to hang a sprig of mistletoe,
you had to shoot it down from the tree. Summers,
with so much dense proliferation at the horizon,
the eye was caught by weed and bush, grapes
sprawling on a low fence, hedgerows of wild rose
or privet hedge, a snarl of honeysuckle, blackberry
along the red gash the road made, and kudzu overtaking
the banks, the rotting logs, a burnt-out barn.
But in winter, from a distance, scanning the hills,
you could easily spot a clump of mistletoe
in the high oak, the topmost branches—
like a nest against the gray sky,
and closer, the only green thing left in the black tree.
After Advent, having tied the wreath of running cedar
and whacked a blue-tipped cedar out of the field;
having unearthed the white potatoes and the yams
and brought the pears and peaches off their shelf;
having sweated all the sugar from the sorghum
and plucked the doves; having long since
slaughtered the hog and swung it by the heels in a nearby tree,
boiled and scraped the bristles, slabbed the ribs,
packed the hams in salt, rinsed and stuffed the gut,
plunged the knuckles into brine, having eaten the testicles
and ground the snout with any remaining parts to make a cheese,
you went upcountry with your gun.
                              O mild Christ,
now everyone is gathered. The parents
quarreling with their one remaining son,
sisters locked in cruel competition—the centerpiece

on the wide plank table is pyracantha, thorn of fire,
torn from a low shrub beside the house.
And lifted above us: emblem of peace, emblem of affection,
with its few pearls, its small inedible berry.

The Photograph

Black as a crow's wing was what they said
about my mother's hair. Even now,
back home, someone on the street
will stop me to recall my mother,
how beautiful she was,
first among her sisters.
In the photograph, her hair
is a spill of ink below the white beret,
a swell of dark water. And her eyes as dark,
her chin lifted, that brusque defining posture
she had just begun in her defense.
Seventeen, on her own,
still a shadow in my father's longing—nothing
the camera could record foretold
her restlessness, the years of shrill
unspecified despair, the clear reproach
of my life, just beginning.

The horseshoe hung in the neck of the tree sinks
deeper into heartwood every season.
Sometimes I hear the past
hum in my ear, its cruel perfected music,
as I turn from the stove
or stop to braid my daughter's thick black hair.

The Riders

He asks for little, so great
is his despair. At the crest
of the white hill, he waits
near the fire, holding the reins
of his expensive sled. The girls
giggle and flirt, winding and unwinding
their patterned scarves—a grown man
wants their attention. One of them
finally edges toward him,
as other children appear
and disappear, plying the hill.
There is no moon, his face
is lit by snow. Although she cannot
name what she feels, already
she understands the terms
of these arrangements:
from her, a rudimentary kindness,
and in exchange, the polished track,
the dull self falling away.

The Chosen

1

You cannot see the horns from where you sit,
only another row in common black.
When their clear melody
comes in to represent a grieving heart,
it will do so as a brook, rushing over stones,
approximates a flock of birds rising,
or as the peacock sounds like human speech.
Now the empty instruments
are raised. I open the first cadenza,
the weight of my arms and shoulders
striking the keys, keys in turn
hammering the hidden strings,
driving triumph from the concert grand:
and when the multiple voices join, when the horns,
in that famous passage, surprise you, it seems
we've touched the vocal center of the world.
The audience a blur on my right,
musicians on my left, I face into the wings,
across the keyboard and its broad extension.
Playing, I have no more choices
to be made. Playing,
I am no one.

2

A child sits on the round, embroidered stool,
screwed to its full height, a box
over the pedals for her feet.
The wooden lip is raised and she taps
at the row of teeth. Suddenly, a passage
from memory, and a bird startles
into its territorial cry; then
she hesitates, tries an accidental—
this is the hard part, the new part—
she doesn't like to make mistakes.
Thinking his opinion matters,
the teacher clicks the rhythm
with a pencil, but I would like
to move those fingers by remote control,
to make her go ahead, take a chance,
play *something*. The piano itself
seems to grow impatient, waiting,
as the tired upright waited for me
in the damp Victorian parlor, a secret
under its fringed shawl, the songs
in the fat book almost in reach—

3

I didn't simply stop getting better.
Pushing a stone, one cannot stop on a hill.
The dancer's legs, the poised embouchure
want to be part of a sleeping animal.

I can still name the train's declining note,
the pitch growing flat as it recedes;
on the street, in a crowd, I can duplicate
the chord implied beneath a random noise—

so much music in the universe!
In the practice halls, or in the deadened
air of their small carrels, apart from us,
musicians are laboring, themselves
the instruments—
                       it is a service;
and like the tired wife who never meant
to foreswear her chosen joy, I merely
gave a lesser portion of myself,

poco a poco until my hands
no longer strained against the leash; and then
no longer could outrun my eye; and soon, soon,
I could not even bear to listen.

The Trust

Something was killing sheep
but it was sheep this dog attended on the farm—
a black-and-white border collie, patrolling his fold
like a parish priest. The second time the neighbor came,
claiming to have spotted the dog at night, a crouched figure
slithering toward the pen on the far side of the county,
the farmer let him witness how the dog,
alert and steady, mended the frayed
edge of the flock, the clumped sheep calm
as they drifted together along the stony hill.
But still more sheep across the glen were slaughtered,
and the man returned more confident. This time,
the master called his dog forward,
and stroking the eager head, prized open the mouth to find,
wound around the base of the back teeth—squat molars
the paws can't reach to clean—small coils of wool,
fine and stiff, like threads from his own jacket.
So he took down the rifle from the rack
and shot the dog and buried him,
his best companion in the field for seven years.
Once satisfied, the appetite is never dulled again.
Night after night, its sweet insistent promise
drives the animal under the rail fence and miles away
for a fresh kill; and with guilty cunning brings him back
to his familiar charges, just now stirring in the early light,
brings him home to his proud husbandry.

The Farmer

In the still-blistering late afternoon,
like currying a horse the rake
circled the meadow, the cut grass ridging
behind it. This summer, if the weather held,
he'd risk a second harvest after years
of reinvesting, leaving fallow.
These fields were why he farmed—
he walked the fenceline like a man in love.
The animals were merely what he needed:
cattle and pigs; chickens for a while; a drayhorse,
saddle horses he was paid to pasture—
an endless stupid round
of animals, one of them always hungry, sick, lost,
calving or farrowing, or waiting slaughter.

When the field began dissolving in the dusk,
he carried feed down to the knoll,
its clump of pines, gate, trough, lick, chute
and two gray hives; leaned into the Jersey's side
as the galvanized bucket filled with milk;
released the cow and turned to the bees.
He'd taken honey before without protection.
This time, they could smell something
in his sweat—fatigue? impatience,
although he was a stubborn, patient man?
Suddenly, like flame, they were swarming over him.
He rolled in the dirt, manure and stiff hoof-prints,
started back up the path, rolled in the fresh hay—
refused to run, which would have pumped

the venom through him faster—passed the oaks
at the yard's edge, rolled in the yard, reached
the kitchen, and when he tore off his clothes
crushed bees dropped from him like scabs.

For a week he lay in the darkened bedroom.
The doctor stopped by twice a day—
the hundred stings "enough to kill an ox,
enough to kill a younger man." What saved him
were the years of smaller doses—
like minor disappointments,
instructive poison, something he could use.

A Song

Now I am calm. It seems that nothing
can make me feel the same exhausting pain.

What is another's harrowing to me?
Grief is not a lake,

I am miles at sea, miles
from the moving figures—

Why are they calling out?
They cluster at land's edge as though

the stony promontory,
where they had just been standing,

were sheared away.
If they are frightened,

if they also grieve,
let them comfort one another,

I cannot help them, I am riding
each enormous wave of this absence

that knows no further shore.

Short Story

My grandfather killed a mule with a hammer,
or maybe with a plank, or a stick, maybe
it was a horse—the story varied
in the telling. If he was planting corn
when it happened, it was a mule, and he was plowing
the upper slope, west of the house, his overalls
stiff to the knees with red dirt, the lines
draped behind his neck.
He must have been glad to rest
when the mule first stopped mid-furrow;
looked back at where he'd come, then down
to the brush along the creek he meant to clear.
No doubt he noticed the hawk's great leisure
over the field, the crows lumped
in the biggest elm on the opposite hill.
After he'd wiped his hatbrim with his sleeve,
he called to the mule as he slapped the line
along its rump, clicked and whistled.

My grandfather was a slight, quiet man,
smaller than most women, smaller
than his wife. Had she been in the yard,
seen him heading toward the pump now,
she'd pump for him a dipper of cold water.
Walking back to the field, past the corncrib,
he took an ear of corn to start the mule,
but the mule was planted. He never cursed
or shouted, only whipped it, the mule
rippling its backside each time

the switch fell, and when that didn't work
whipped it low on its side, where it's tender,
then cross-hatched the welts he'd made already.
The mule went down on one knee,
and that was when he reached for the blown limb,
or walked to the pile of seasoning lumber; or else,
unhooked the plow and took his own time to the shed
to get the hammer.

              By the time I was born,
he couldn't even lift a stick. He lived
another fifteen years in a chair,
but now he's dead, and so is his son,
who never meant to speak a word against him,
and whom I never asked what his father
was planting and in which field,
and whether it happened before he married,
before his children came in quick succession,
before his wife died of the last one.
And only a few of us are left
who ever heard that story.

Stone Pond

Driving over the limit
on a mountain road,
the mist rising, Stone Pond
white with ice and white mist
inside its circle
of birch and black fir:

driving home after
seeing friends, the radio
complicitous and loud,
Beethoven's braided musical line,
a sonata I recall
playing well:

passing the tiny houses
on the hillside, woodsmoke
rising among the budded trees,
then passing within inches
of someone's yard:
I circle Stone Pond, and despair

seems like something I can set aside.
The road bends again, the morning
burns through the mist.
Sufficient joy—
what should I have done to make it last?

II

The Visitor

Every summer, after the slender dogwood by the porch
has dropped its scalloped blossoms, my sister
moves back into the carcass of our house.
Most of the old belongings are disbursed,
most of the photographs, the lamps, the quilts,
the small unraveling stool.
And there's a different smell—
Some other kind of soap in the yellow bathroom,
some other dish simmering on the stove.
Upstairs, in the room we shared,
wasps crawl undisturbed across the pane.
Still, my sister says
she feels my father's presence everywhere—
among the trees and bushes he had planted,
the billiard-cloth of grass she cuts and mends.
After midnight, he turns the light on
in the living room; and once, at his usual waking,
before daybreak could have lit the kitchen,
she heard his spoon chime against his cup.
But not my mother—
not on the glassed-in porch,
not beside the single strand of roses.

My sister thinks it's natural that she comes,
that she stays through August, keeping up
the hardwood floors. Away from her grown children
she sings in the choir, empties another closet,
cultivates the bluebirds in their boxes.
When she calls, her news is either weather

or the birds, it is so quiet there.
But sometimes I hear her hesitate on the phone,
as though to tell me something, or to ask—

Then she is adult again, reports
a new house on the road and more trees cleared.
"Try to get home," is what she says,
the closed vowel encompassing
our set of inland islands: ragged plug
of the Southern map, the house and yard
centered in the green voluptuous fields,
and all of my childhood, pocked reef
floating within me, relic of past eruption
now cooled, now temperate, populous, isolate,
from which I venture further and further
into this life, like a swimmer
still in training, aiming
for the mainland in the distance.

The Wide and Varied World

Women, women, what do they want?

The first ones in the door of the plant-filled office
were the twins, fresh from the upper grades,
their matched coats dangling open.
And then their more compliant brother, leading
the dear stuffed tottering creature—amazing
that she could lift her leg high enough
to cross the threshold to the waiting room.
Then the woman, the patient, carrying the baby
in an infant seat, his every inch of flesh
swaddled against the vicious weather.
Once inside, how skillfully the mother
unwound the many layers—

                and now so quickly
must restore them: news from the lab
has passed through the nurse's sliding window.
The youngest, strapped again into his shell,
fusses for the breast, the twins tease their sister,
the eight-year-old looks almost wise as his mother
pinches his sweaty neck, her hissed threats
swarming his face like flies.

                Now she's gone.
The women who remain don't need to speak.
Outside, snow falls in the streets
and quiet hills, and seems, in the window,
framed by the room's continuous greenery,
to obliterate the wide and varied world.
We half-smile, half-nod to one another.
One returns to her magazine.

One shifts gently to the right arm
her sleeping newborn, unfurls the bud of its hand.
One of us takes her turn in the inner office
where she submits to the steel table
and removes from her body its stubborn wish.
We want what you want, only
we have to want it more.

The Field Trip

This time they're thirteen, no longer
interested in the trillium on the path but in each other,
though they will not say so. Only the chaperone
lingers at the adder's-tongue,
watching the teacher trail the rest uphill
to where the dense virginal forest thins and opens.
At the clearing, she tells them to be still and mute
and make a list of what they see and hear.
A girl asks if she should also list
the way she feels—she's the one
who'll cite the shadow on the lake below.
The others sprawl on gender-separate rocks
except for the smart-ass, perched
on the cliff-edge, inviting front-page photos—
PICNIC MARRED BY TRAGEDY. From time to time,
in the midst of the day's continual lunch,
as the students read the lists their teacher edits,
the boy swears and stretches—
he is in fact fourteen, doing seventh grade
a second time, this same assignment
also a second time. Pressed, he says
he sees exactly what he saw before—ponds, rocks, trees—
shouting it back from the same vantage point
out on the twelve-inch ledge,
Long Pond a ragged puddle underneath him;
and what he shouts grows more and more
dangerously insubordinate as he leans
more and more dramatically over the edge.
But he is, after all, the first to spot the hawk;

and it is, looking down on it, amazing. The others
gather near the unimpeded view,
together, finally, standing on this bluff
overlooking three natural ponds, hearing the wind
ruffle the cedar fringe, watching the hawk
float along the thermals like a leaf.
And for a moment, belittled by indifferent wilderness,
you want to praise the boy, so much does he resemble
if not the hawk then the doomed shrub
fanned against the rockface there beside him,
rooted in a fissure in the rock.
But soon the hero swings back up to earth,
the group divides. Just like that
they're ready for home, tired of practicing:
sixteen children, two adults, and one
bad boy who carved a scorpion on his arm.

Nocturne

Through the clotted street and down
the alley to the station, the halting
rhythm of the bus disrupts her dream
and makes the broad blond fields of grain
yield to an agitated harbor,
whales nuzzling flank to flank.
Now the bus settles in its gate.
She wakes, smoothes her stockings, gathers
her packages; a nervous woman,
she passes the subway's deep stairs
and aims for the Public Garden: a few ducks
in the shallow murk of the pond, a few bikes,
the labeled trees, the low voltage of the pigeons' moan,
the last light doled out to penthouses on the roofline
where someone shifts an ottoman with his slipper.
This is not the red heart of the city
but its veined, unblinking eye,
her image fixed within the green iris.
Across the avenue, up the blank side street,
the door is locked, those locks her talisman.
She stalls a moment, as a cautious animal pauses
before it is absorbed by foliage—she is alone at dusk
in the emptying corridors of the park. Nearby
a man flattens the clipped grass.
He knows each coin, the currency of faces.
Trailing her from the bus, deft as a cab
in the dense streets, as a dog on the broad common,
he's neither hungry nor afraid, a man with a knife
evolving coolly from the traffic of strangers.

Whereas the violence in nature is just,
beasts taking their necessary flesh,
the city is capricious, releasing brute
want from the body's need where it was housed.

Fairy Tale

The wronged spirit brought the child
a basket of riches:
two parents, justice and mercy;
a beauty both stunning and organic;
fame beyond the wide walls of the castle;
and intelligence, lying like an asp
at the bottom of the basket.
With this last gift she could discern
the flaw in nature
and all of nature's fruits.

Thus she came to her
majority already skilled,
having pressed bright flowers
to a film, having memorized
the verses of the day.
For months, she did not eat,
she did not traffic with the agencies
of change: she had cast her will entirely

against decay. Even when
the wild tangle emerged
from the careful lawns, and ebony birds
came down from the woods
to roost in the chiseled turrets
and foul the court, she would not stir
nor in any way disturb
the triumph that would greet the shallow prince:
a soul unencumbered
in a neutral body.

Under Gemini

This morning, as if striping the lower field
were not enough, sun flooded the south windows
at an angle, dissolving the glass
dividing the plants inside from plants outside
where almost all that blooms is blooming.
So finally I opened all the doors,
unstoppered the upstairs windows and swept away
the delicate crisp husks of flies, the dark
accumulation of the winter. And now
you're splashing the children
with the hose, urging me out into the sun,
as I sit in the shade of the porch under the eaves
where spiders do their work—
symmetrical hammocks and flannel sacks of eggs.
Have you noticed they always move
in increments, from bush to tree to post:
even when they fly, they fall on a tether or make
a lateral swing in the wind—unlike birds, light-bellied
swallows with forked tails and ruddered swifts, descending
from the barn in open air, free-fall, snatching
flies on the wing—summer calls us
to be birds, calls us to abandon.
When Orpheus heard the mermaids sing, he sang louder.
It's right that I wait here with the spiders
growing larger, slower, shrewder
at the target's edge.

Good News

Not smart, not pretty, not especially kind,
one of a million sparrows in God's eye,
she sits in the middle pew this hot
second Sunday in July, All Day Meeting
and eating on the grounds. Home for the day,
wearing a fuchsia dress and precarious smile
she looks somehow fallen but unused,
a peony dismantling on the bush.
As the preacher chides and harrows his drowsy flock
she studies the large mural spread behind him:
their savior dressed in light; eleven choral faces;
and one who's looking, always, down and away.
Through the open door, the open windows
with leaded hillsides flecked with sheep,
no breeze comes in from heaven
to stir the damp curls along her neck
so she moves her paper fan with the languorous
motion of the wrist a Fiji Islander
might use to sway a frond—

                          Outside, a bird
flutes among the lilies. The cobbled tables
stand between the white church and the graves,
nothing left of chicken and pie, biscuits and lemonade,
nothing left of the women who dished it up
in feathered hats, or the men in shirtsleeves
with their braces showing, boys chasing beneath the oaks
and girls in white piqué and patent shoes, their hair
already wet from the blessed river—as if snatched
out of the yard, they've gone inside

to blink and nod, and swept among them,
this almost unfamiliar single woman, who rustled
from group to group, balancing a tiny plate of food.
Near her, in the aisle, as though arranged,
a thick fluorescent bug struggles and whirs.
And below the windows' many fractured Christs,
the broad metal fans that stir the ceiling, she sees
it isn't dawn in the painting, as she thought,
but dusk and deepening gloom,

                              as now, in the church,
where the widow to her right with strict gray hair,
the deacons and the choir are standing, the hymn
is gathering speed and urgency, everybody's
singing out for Jesus! The preacher
punctuates the crowd with invitation—Jesus!
Who has saved the sullen grocer at the back,
a farmer and his wife, a naughty child—
Jesus!—and they file forward, happy to be chosen,
but still the preacher's murmuring,
Jesus with the leper, Jesus weeping.
His brow is cool and calm; he has the poor
lost disciple's darkened face, he has the lean
body of the boy who boxes fruit, he holds the only
key to the grave, and she is lovely, rising now,
descending the aisle toward the one who loves her.

Amaryllis

Having been a farmer's daughter
she didn't want to be a farmer's wife, didn't want
the smell of ripe manure in all his clothes,
the corresponding flies in her kitchen,
a pail of slop below the sink,
a crate of baby chicks beside the stove, piping
beneath their bare lightbulb, cows calling at the gate
for him to come, cows standing in the chute
as he crops their horns with his long sharp shears.
So she nagged him toward a job in town;
so she sprang from the table, weeping, when he swore;
so, after supper, she sulks over her mending
as he unfolds his pearl pocketknife
to trim a callus on his palm.
Too much like her mother, he says, not knowing
any other reason why she spoils the children,
or why he comes in from the combine with his wrenches
to find potatoes boiled dry in their pot,
his wife in the parlor on the bench
at her oak piano—not playing
you understand, just sitting like a fern
in that formal room.
                    So much time to think,
these long hours: like her mother,
each night she goes to bed when her husband's tired,
gets up when he gets up, and in between tries
not to move, listening to the sleep of this good man
who lies beside and over her. So much time alone,
since everything he knows is practical.

Just this morning, he plunged an icepick
into the bloated side of the cow unable to rise,
dying where it fell, its several stomachs having failed—
too full, he said, of sweet wet clover.

Nightshade

The dog lay under the house, having crawled
back beyond the porch, bellying
beneath the joists through rocks and red dirt
to the cool stone foundation where it died
as the children called and sobbed;
and now their father had to wrench it out,
the one he had been breaking to handle birds.

This was a man of strictest moderation,
who had heard a dash of strychnine in its meat
could be a tonic for a dog, an extra edge.
He loved that dog, and got the dosage wrong.
And I loved my father—
I was among the children looking on—
and for years would not forgive him:

without pure evil in the world,
there was no east or west, no polestar
and no ratifying dove. I sat inside
the small white house for hours,
deaf to the world, playing my two songs,
one in a major, the other in a sad, minor key.

At the Movie: Virginia, 1956

This is how it was:
they had their own churches, their own schools,
school buses, football teams, bands and majorettes,
separate restaurants, in all the public places
their own bathrooms, at the doctor's
their own waiting room, in the *Tribune*
a column for their news, in the village
a neighborhood called Sugar Hill,
uneven rows of unresponsive houses
that took the maids back in each afternoon—
in our homes used the designated door,
on Trailways sat in the back, and at the movie
paid at a separate entrance, stayed upstairs.
Saturdays, a double feature drew the local kids
as the town bulged, families surfacing
for groceries, medicine and wine,
the black barber, white clerks in the stores—crowds
lined the sidewalks, swirled through the courthouse yard,
around the stone soldier and the flag,

and still I never *saw* them on the street.
It seemed a chivalric code
laced the milk: you'd try not to look
and they would try to be invisible.
Once, on my way to the creek,
I went without permission to the tenants'
log cabin near the barns, and when Aunt Susie
opened the door, a cave yawned, and beyond her square,
leonine, freckled face, in the hushed interior,

Joe White lumbered up from the table, six unfolding
feet of him, dark as a gun-barrel, his head bent
to clear the chinked rafters, and I caught
the terrifying smell of sweat and grease,
smell of the woodstove, night jar, straw mattress—

This was rural Piedmont, upper south;
we lived on a farm but not in poverty.
When finally we got our own TV, the evening news
with its hooded figures of the Ku Klux Klan
seemed like another movie—*King Solomon's Mines*,
the serial of Atlantis in the sea.
By then I was thirteen,
and no longer went to movies to see movies.
The downstairs forged its attentions forward,
toward the lit horizon, but leaning a little
to one side or the other, arranging the pairs
that would own the county, stores and farms, everything
but easy passage out of there—
and through my wing-tipped glasses the balcony
took on a sullen glamor: whenever the film
sputtered on the reel, when the music died
and the lights came on, I swiveled my face
up to where they whooped and swore,
to the smoky blue haze and that tribe
of black and brown, licorice, coffee,
taffy, red oak, sweet tea—

wanting to look, not knowing how to see,
I thought it was a special privilege
to enter the side door, climb the stairs
and scan the even rows below—trained bears
in a pit, herded by the stringent rule,
while they were free, lounging above us,
their laughter pelting down on us like trash.

The Storm

After trimming the split trunk of our tallest maple,
we drove along the cluttered road to see
the other damage. On the next high ground,
the neighbors' white frame house was still intact
but their porch was lined in black—like silk, that soft
when we touched it—a jagged hole where the switch box
used to be, where lightning entered. Indoors,
it had traced a map on the walls
as it traveled the wires behind the walls,
throwing out at every socket fists of fire only inches
from where they sat. No one had been hurt, no one
shocked or burned, but each needed
to tell us what had happened, still figuring
whether to count their luck as bad or good.

We took the long way back to check the creek
loosened from its channel into the fields,
crowding the cattle to an upper ridge,
the young sycamores along the bank
shorter now by half, forking
at water level, and the water red as rust,
swift, swirling the whipped limbs of the willow oaks,
grazing the concrete bridge and full of trash.
My father explained the bloated lumps
as logs, or broken fence, and pointed out
occasional shimmering arrows at the surface—
something alive and swimming with the current—

trying to make it all seem natural,
as my mother had calmed us
in the noise and flash and passion
we'd shuddered through the night before.
But already a smell was rising from the new river,
the bottomland, the small lost animals it swallowed.
And we were learning risk and consequence:
in the neighbors' yard
strips of rubber draping trees and grass,
the poles unattached, the central silver cord
simply missing, that carried power in.

The Cusp

So few birds—the ones that winter through
and the geese migrating through the empty fields,
fording the cropped, knuckled stalks of corn:
all around us, all that's green's suppressed,
and in the brooding wood, the bare trees,
shorn of leaves or else just shy of leaves,
make a dark estate beneath low clouds
that have the look of stubborn snow.

In a purely scientific exercise—
say you came from the moon, or returned
like Lazarus, blinking from the cave—
you wouldn't know if winter's passed or now beginning.
The bank slopes up, the bank slopes down to the ditch.
Would it help if I said grieving has an end?
Would it matter if I told you this is spring?

The Pendulum

One-third of the house is hanging in the air,
or seems to hang, seems ready to buckle
the six slender jacks underneath—we had to correct
two hundred years of shifting on this hill,
the sills laid in sand and left there, four warped timbers
that frame us as we sleep, frost
pressing every winter on every wall, so far away
from the mild Virginia evenings, the doves calling softly
in the field, and my childhood house, its mild human voices.
In June, in my garden, hearing a dove
across the wooded swell—the first I'd heard
in this northern latitude—I realized that nothing
is left to pull me back there but the graves; and like an exile
finally turning inland from the shore, I could admit
I'm here to stay.
                        So we exposed the rotten wood
from outside in, the vast machine laboring in the yard,
its prehistoric hand surprisingly agile, tender; and at night
can feel that end of the house
shuddering up to pitch on the iron rods, as though we had
released it, had removed the weights from the swimmer's feet;
and the awful dreams have started once again, although
I wake to find the children undisturbed. Do they know
how soon the dirt mounded on the grass
will be shoveled back against the new foundation,
the cellarhole tucked in? Already, stone by stone
the Polish mason sets us right—not on the earth
but in it, level where the land is not,
squared where it slopes away and plumb to a rule, the line

that ties this planet to its star: a line made visible
by the string he hangs from the underside of the house,
its dependent metal cone an ornament, a pendulum
that sways, slows, grows perfectly still
to mark the footings here, and here, and here.

Frog

can't help herself, goes in and out of water
all day long. The reed wags like a finger,
the slick patch of algae shrugs and stretches—
Make up your mind.
They have the luxury of just one life.
Frog would like to venture into the weeds, or further still,
but her skin dries, too much open air is like a poison.
Underwater, confident again, Frog
keeps her legs together
to imitate the missing tail, circles the long trout,
plunges down to sweet familiar ooze.
But Frog is always too soon out of breath
and must return to the bright element
where the other land-fish line the banks,
huge and slow, picking their teeth. Close by,
in the blurred trees, new rivals have been hatching.
Frog takes up her perch where the linked bubbles
decorate the wet hem of the pond.
She sits and sits, like a clod of grass, her eyeballs
fixed and glassy, the slim tongue uncurls, curls
in her mouth: although she cannot fly
she eats what does. And then,
staring down into her losses, into the pool
that swaddled her among her mute companions,
Frog fills her throat with air and sings.

III

The Waterfall

Meeting after twenty years apart,
I ask my friend to give me back myself
at nineteen, but he can't, or won't:
Sunny, he says, and quick to speak your mind.
Then he asks if he has aged,
if he looks the same—who had always seemed
so satisfied, past need, past harm.
At every stop we stare at each other,
returning to the other's face as though
it were a wind-rucked pond we hope will clear.
And slowly, as we spiral up the mountain,
looking for landmarks, the road
a narrow shelf on the wooded slopes, I realize
he's terrified of me; and since he cannot yet
know who I am, begin to see myself as I was then:
implacable:

              but that's not the word he flung at me
beside the shaded pool, the blanket smoothed,
the picnic barely opened. That was years ago;
now we have the usual pleasantries,
trade photographs, his family and mine,
their fixed improbable faces.

                    Eventually,
we find the general store, the left-turn fork,
the hidden waterfall still
battering the rocks,
and the ease of recognition makes me old.
Standing close enough to feel the spray,
looking up at the falls, its powerful

inexhaustible rush of water,
I think that art has ruined my life,
fraught as it is with what's exceptional.
But that's not true; at the start, at nineteen,
I wanted it all,
every exhilaration, every grief—

acquisitive was what he said.
How could I have hurt him?
Such a new candle, just lit, burning, burning.

Memorial Day

In field guides they are always in repose:
tiny female, olive-gray, so like the local birds;
the male, shiny black with tail stripes, wing bars,
"shoulder coloration" such a vivid orange
I might have recognized him in the elm.
But this close—for days, midday, over and over
they sprang from the nearest branch of the shrub,
slinging themselves at the glass, then hovering there
with so much apparent purpose my son said,
Why don't you open the window and let them in?

For a moment, it was the voice of clearest reason.
And it must have been the same for the early fishermen
on the Klamath River, after
the terrible dark winters of retribution,
seeing the water clot with fish and fish twist
willingly into their nets, who thought the salmon
had been sent to feed them and their families—
hadn't they prayed steadily, and weren't the fish
laboring upstream?
                    Likewise, my father's cousin,
deep in the mud and confusion of the war,
heard a woman's voice, distinct
as a mouth harp, his dead wife's voice,
urging him out of the foxhole, out of the path
of the sudden German shell that killed the others.
And now, two rare impatient birds flying at me, erect,
sun-struck, treading the air, their mouths propped
open as if to speak, as if they were not birds

but messengers—
                    but I am overrun with signs and omens:
the pair death has taken
swim up like motes in my eye, I find them
everywhere I look, I put them there; it is a blindness.
American redstart warblers. If they have meaning, perhaps
they represent the living, not the dead;
and I am meant to understand
death is locked behind the glass
that teases with our own reflections
until the implicating sun moves to the southwest
and the window once again holds only shadow.

It's been a week since their last visitation.
At the window, the smudge of purple,
those small rich berries the buds made,
has opened into the blossoms'
distinguishing pastel, a thicket of lilac.
From time to time I catch among the usual calls
a sequence of notes—not a warble at all but abrupt
chips of sound—to match the guide's
approximating graph, which records,
though it cannot translate, what they say.

The Wish

My daughter comes to me
with her sorrow. She is
not yet ten, not yet
insistent for her father.
As if waiting out a sentence,
she sits at the round table,
her long black shawl of hair
framing high cheekbones.
She thinks she is ugly,
thinks she has no friends.

How can I comfort, what should I
try to tell this radiant
coincidence of genes?
That children can be beasts
to one another? That envy
eats us from the inside?
"All great beauties
doubted their beauty," I tell her.
But why should she believe me:
I am her mother, and asked
repeatedly for beauty,
meaning happiness.

Bright Leaf

Like words put to a song, the bunched tobacco leaves
are strung along a stick, the women
standing in the August heat for hours—since first light—
under the pitched tin roof, barefoot, and at their feet
the babies, bare-assed, dirty, eating dirt.
The older children hand the leaves from the slide,
three leaves at a time, stalks upright, three handers
for each stringer, and three more heaped canvas slides
waiting in what little shade there is: it's ten o'clock,
almost dinnertime. They pull the pails of cold lunch
and Mason jars of tea out of the spring
when they see the farmer coming from the field, their men
stripped to the waist, polished by sweat and tired as mules.
By afternoon, the loose cotton dresses, even
the headrags are dark with sweat.
Still their fingers never miss a stitch,
though they're paid not by the stick but by the day,
and the talk—unbroken news of cousins and acquaintances—
unwinding with the ball of twine, a frayed snuff-twig
bouncing on one lip, the string paying out
through their calluses, the piles of wide green leaves
diminishing, until the men appear with the last slide
and clamber up the rafters of the barn
to line the loaded sticks along the tiers. It's Friday:

the farmer pays with a wad of ones and fives,
having turned the mule out to its feed and water,
hung up the stiffened traces and the bit. He checks
again the other barns, already fired, crude ovens

of log and mud where the crop is cured;
in that hot dry acrid air, spreads a yellowing leaf
across his palm, rolls an edge in his fingers,
gauging by its texture and its smell
how high to drive the fire.
His crew is quiet in the pickup truck—did you think
they were singing? They are much too tired to even speak,
can barely lick salt from the back of a hand, brush at flies,
hush a baby with a sugartit. And the man
who owns this land is also tired.
Everyday this week he's meant to bring home pears
from the old tree by the barn, but now he sees
the fruit has fallen, sees the yellow jackets feeding there.
He lights a Lucky, frames a joke for his wife—he'll say
their banker raised a piss-poor field this year.
And she will lean against the doorjamb
while he talks, while he scrubs his hands at the tin basin
with a split lemon and a pumice stone, rubs them raw
trying to cut the gummy resin, that stubborn
black stain within the green.

The Fence

Think of it as a target's outer edge—
the bands of lawn, gravel, lawn,
the red brick bull's-eye of the house.
Dead center was the kitchen, whose windows opened
a view of the yard, the trees and bushes
newly planted, each in its small depression,
and the more ambitious birds—
cardinal, blue jay, mockingbird—
tagging the older trees beside the fence.
Along one flank of the yard, that meant mimosa,
a pink canopy, silk blossoms shaped
like downy parasols; and it was here
she taught herself to move beyond the branches
onto the edge, inching down the planks
around the house. When she fell
she fell inward, away from the field.
But once in the air and moving forward,
she was neither in the yard nor in the field,
balanced over hay and broom,
the dried plates of dung and piles
still liquid, green as infection, the hidden
nests of snakes or rabbits, and the obvious cows,
wearing their stockings of offal, lurching and switching.
How easily the world was once divided. In the field
the doves cried in their private tunnels of grass,
and beyond, her father's pasture gave way
to woods and creek, the high trestle,
someone else's woods and creek. She knew
who was supposed to be the sun, who the moon,

who the pebble under the skirt of the moon.
By summer's end, doubling her own height,
she'd traced the whole decorative length of wood
around the house to the corner by the road
where fence was used to keep things in, not out.
And that is how I see her even now—
not yet straining against a tether but held erect
by the gravitational pull from either side—
face forward, arms extended, headed for the far post
where wood turned into wire.

Equinox

The garden slackens under frost,
and the trees, scored by the season's extravagant
orange and red, begin discarding
what they will not need.
How many more signals do we want?
Brown, gray, the brown skittery refuse in the field
is what the natural world is moving toward.
In the middle distance,
the children run to the creek,
run to the dwarf-apple and across
the clipped green grass to where their father
is stacking wood, all of them wearing primary blue.
This yard is what we salvage from the scrub
that overtakes the orchard and the pasture.
Perennial. The earth mocks us,
and in the blue heavens,
nothing visible
but her pale oblivious twin.

Landscape, Dense with Trees

When you move away, you see how much depends
on the pace of the days—how much
depended on the haze we waded through
each summer, visible heat, wavy and discursive
as the lazy track of the snake in the dusty road;
and on the habit in town of porches thatched in vines,
and in the country long dense promenades, the way
we sacrificed the yards to shade.
It was partly the heat that made my father
plant so many trees—two maples marking the site
for the house, two elms on either side when it was done;
mimosa by the fence, and as it failed, fast-growing chestnuts,
loblolly pines; and dogwood, redbud, ornamental crab.
On the farm, everything else he grew
something could eat, but this
would be a permanent mark of his industry,
a glade established in the open field. Or so it seemed.
Looking back at the empty house from across the hill,
I see how well the house is camouflaged, see how
that porous fence of saplings, their later
scrim of foliage, thickened around it,
and still he chinked and mortared, planting more.
Last summer, although he'd lost all tolerance for heat,
he backed the truck in at the family grave
and stood in the truckbed all afternoon, pruning
the landmark oak, repairing recent damage by a wind;
then he came home and hung a swing
in one of the horse-chestnuts for my visit.
The heat was a hand at his throat,

a fist to his weak heart. But it made a triumph
of the cooler air inside, in the bedroom,
in the maple bedstead where he slept,
in the brick house nearly swamped by leaves.

The Lotus Flowers

The surface of the pond was mostly green—
bright green algae reaching out from the banks,
then the mass of waterlilies, their broad round leaves
rim to rim, each white flower spreading
from the center of a green saucer.
We teased and argued, choosing the largest,
the sweetest bloom, but when the rowboat
lumbered through and rearranged them,
we found the plants were anchored, the separate
muscular stems descending in the dense water—
only the most determined put her hand
into that frog-slimed pond
to wrestle with a flower. Back and forth
we pumped across the water, in twos and threes,
full of brave adventure. On the marshy shore,
the others hollered for their turns,
or at the hem of where we pitched the tents
gathered firewood—
                    this was wilderness,
although the pond was less than half an acre
and we could still see the grand magnolias
in the village cemetery, their waxy
white conical blossoms gleaming in the foliage.
A dozen girls, the oldest only twelve, two sisters
with their long braids, my shy neighbor,
someone squealing without interruption:
all we didn't know about the world buoyed us,
as the frightful water sustained and moved the flowers
tethered at a depth we couldn't see.

In the late afternoon, before they'd folded
into candles on the dark water,
I went to fill the bucket at the spring.
Deep in the pines, exposed tree roots
formed a natural arch, a cave of black loam.
I raked off the skin of leaves and needles,
leaving a pool so clear and shallow
I could count the pebbles
on the studded floor. The sudden cold
splashing up from the bucket to my hands
made me want to plunge my hand in—
and I held it under, feeling the shock that wakes
and deadens, watching first my fingers,
then the ledge beyond me,
the snake submerged and motionless,
the head propped on its coils the way a girl
crosses her arms before her on the sill
and rests her chin there.
                            Lugging the bucket
back to the noisy clearing, I found nothing changed,
the boat still rocked across the pond,
the fire straggled and cracked as we fed it
branches and debris into the night,
leaning back on our pallets—
spokes in a wheel—learning the names of the many
constellations, learning how each fixed
cluster took its name:
not from the strongest light, but from the pattern
made by stars of lesser magnitude,
so like the smaller stars we rowed among.

May

Raccoons on the porch, the deer
leaving stenciled hearts
in the soft ground beneath the apple tree—
yesterday Will announced
"a wild and beautiful goose" up the brook.
I thought it must have been a duck
but today, looking out the back window
toward the stream, I see
what I take to be a pile of trash
until it moves—
                    there is a goose,
preening its long neck, its orange lips
grazing among the cress and mown grass,
though for minutes at a time it doesn't move.

In the painting that our yard would be,
the blunt white goose pulls the eye
from the white circle of the blossoming tree—
it lights the tree,
as if its smaller swatch of white
conjured brilliance out of the shadowed grass.

One by one I call the others;
we stand together, watching, in a hush.
And so it is
when the dog drags home the plush
hindquarter of a deer; or when
a single beaver sits beside the barn,
holding up his paws like a friendly dog.

Dancing with Poets

"The accident" is what he called the time
he threw himself from a window four floors up,
breaking his back and both ankles so that walking
became the direst labor for this man
who takes my hand, invites me to the empty strip of floor
that fronts the instruments, a length of polished wood
the shape of a grave. *Unsuited for this world:*
his body bears the marks of it, his hand
is tense with effort and with shame, and I shy away
from any audience, but I love to dance—and soon
we find a way to move, drifting apart as each
effects a different ripple across the floor,
a plaid and a stripe to match the solid navy of the band.
And suddenly the band is getting better, so pleased
to have this pair of dancers, since we make evident
the music in the noise—and the dull pulse
leaps with unexpected riffs and turns, we can hear
how good the keyboard really is, the bright cresting
of another major key as others join us: a strict
block of a man, a formidable cliff of mind, dancing
as if melted, as if unhinged; his partner a gift of brave
elegance to those who watch her dance; and at her elbow
Berryman back from the bridge, and Frost, relieved
of grievances, Dickinson waltzing there with lavish Keats,
who coughs into a borrowed handkerchief—all the poets of exile
and despair, unfit for this life, all those who cannot speak
but only sing, all those who cannot walk
who strut and spin until the waiting citizens at the bar,
aloof, judgmental, begin to sway or drum their straws or hum,

leave their seats to crowd the narrow floor
as though we were one body, sweating and foolish,
one body with its clear pathetic grace,
not lifted out of grief but dancing it, transforming
for one night this local bar, before we're turned back out
to our separate selves, to the dangerous streets and houses,
to the overwhelming drone of the living world.

TWO TREES

(1992)

For Lee Hampton Benton

First Song

Having stolen twelve of Apollo's cows
he butchered two: an offering to the gods,
and one for himself, since he was hungry.

Great ugliness defeated, and great evil: the hero
swings the monster's head like a lantern!
But in some accounts, it's only
gentle Hermes in a mask, or sometimes
the serpents are the streamers on his staff.
His task is leading out the newly dead: Shepherd, Augur,
Patron of Thieves, who had once been
Master of Invention,

                   inventing the lyre
from cow-gut and a tortoiseshell,
with which he lulled his mother into sleep;
and the flute, a sheaf of seven reeds,
with which he passed the endless childhood hours;
and games of chance, of skill,
a game of sooth played on knucklebones—
pleasures to woo those who found him
odd, and vain, dismissive
of what came easy,

               as it was easy
charming stiff Apollo and trading up:
for the fruits of his restless solitude
the pouch at his hip, wings at his feet,
a place at the high table—
and now he shuttled in and out of heaven,
bearing the sealed messages:
half a god.

         Like the gods, a youth

with multiple gifts and single-mindedness
can make himself invisible; and this is how
he came, in foulest weather, to the cave,
where the Fates, Triple-Goddess of the Moon,
weave and cut the stories, the human lives,
just one tooth among them,
just one eye:

        with the eye he saw
the magnitude of what he'd thrown away,
who gave the world the musical scale,
sounds become a sweetness and a power;
who gave the world the alphabet,
the mind made supple as the hand;
who gave the world hymns of invocation,
seven vowels uttered in succession,
so mortals might petition
blind fortune;

        and he cast his fortune
when he cast the tooth, and knew
whether those on earth were lost or blest,
beauty would divide them

and each unwind as on a spindle rod
until the blade settles against the thread—
with no more than a flutter in the air
he's there at the bloody couch,
God of Contracts,

        God of Silence,
who lays the golden staff across their eyes.

Effort at Speech

Nothing was as we'd thought, the sea
anemones not plants but animals,
flounder languishing on the sand
like infants waiting to be turned—
from the bottom we followed the spiral ramp
around and up, circling the tank.
Robert, barely out of the crib,
rode his father's shoulders, uttering
words or parts of words and pointing
ceaselessly toward the water, toward
one of the many shapes in the water,
what he could not name, could not describe.
Starfish, monkfish—not fish—catfish,
sea hare, sea horse: we studied the plaques
for something to prompt him with,
but he tucked his head as if shamed.
So I left them at the school of the quick
yellow-with-black-stripes conventional,
passed the armored centenary
turtle going down as I went up,
seaweed, eels, elongate gun-gray suede
bodies of the prehistoric sharks
traversing the reef, and headed to the top,
thinking to look down through the multiple layers.
When it first came at me, it seemed more
creature of the air than of the sea,
huge, delta-winged, bat-winged,
head subsumed in the spread pectorals—
unless it was all head—a kite

gliding to the wall between us, veering
up, over, exposing its light belly,
"face" made by gill-slits opening,
the tail's long whip and poison spine.
Eagle Ray: *cordata*, like the eagle;
it skated along the glass—
eagle scanning the sheer canyon wall,
bat trapped inside the cave,
no, like a mind at work, at play,
I felt I was seeing through the skull—
and then away.

At the Piano

At the piano, the girl, as if rowing upstream,
is driving triplets against the duple meter,
one hand for repetition,
one hand for variation and for song.
She knows nothing, but Bach knows everything.
Outside, in the vast disordered world,
the calves have been taken from their mothers;
both groups bawled and hooted all night long—
she heard them from her quilted double bed.
Twice a day, she gives the young
their frothy warm placebo. While her brother
steadies the cow with grain, her sister
leans in close from the little stool,
fingertips aligned on the wrinkled tits
as if to pick some soft, fleshy fruit
but pressing in, hard, while pulling down,
she milks with both hands, two jets of milk
spraying the metal pail as they go in.
The girl must put her whole hand in the pail
and push the head of the suckling toward it:
wet muzzle, corrugated tongue.
Last year's calf is in the bank. On the mantel,
brass candlesticks, twinned again in the mirror,
and the loud squat clock, her metronome.
At the piano, hands in her lap—
what's given, and what's made from luck and will—
she also hears a diaphonic moan:
long before dusk the animals in the pens
again have started calling for each other,

either hungry or too full, she can't tell
which is which. Her mother's in the kitchen,
her father's in the hayloft pitching hay,
she pushes off in her wooden boat—
she knows nothing, she thinks
no one could be happier than this.

Variations: At the Piano

The almost visible wall
is made of sound.
It keeps the girl apart
as she prefers,
as long as her fingers
press the even keys,
as long as the household
hears the web of sound
spun from the loom.

Outside, in mild
or terrible weather, trees
bud, flower, leaf out,
lose leaves. Inside,
the king and queen have swooned,
the castle swoons.

Wall of glass, of gauze.

True pitch:
when the eye can hear,
when the ear names what's heard:
the mind becomes a second instrument.

Transposing the world to one mathematic *A,*
she envies how the others
steer by the wake of any passing ship.
Fixed to a fixed star, she becomes the star—
that distant—
a flare in the crowded heavens.

The day is foul—a thin sleet falling everywhere,
the slops of it congealing on the street
with trash, soot, smog and general grime,
the sky's dark clouds incarnate underfoot,
buses, cars, people, rats, roaches
flooding the street with their effluvia.
Inside the studio, it's high summer,
eighteenth-century rational Germany.
On the open score a meadow blooms, the notes
flowers on their upright stems, the pianist
harvesting from each its grain of sound—
she has, that is, the undeflected focus
of a bee, and from the concert grand
the fugue emerging—

                    see how it seduces,
what carries no mark of the present world,
no news, no merchants, no murderous weather,
no crude alarms, no lives lost or saved.

"Earthy, exuberant, full of gusto,
bristling with intelligence.

And the tips of your fingers were so very small."
He leans across her arm to pour the wine.

Since thirty years have passed he can admit
he envied her her gifts—

perhaps mistakes that envy for desire,
like David on the throne hearing the harp.

And now remembers the slope of her white neck;
and now is sure that neck's improved with age.

Digging a hole to where the past is buried,
one covers the living grass on either side.

This far inland, after the hurricane,
wind on the porch sufficient
to chuff and ravel the tangled "baby's-tears"
disturbs the cluster of chimes:
five separate oriental tones
in endless permutations—both pattern and not pattern—
as the central lozenge is stirred to strike
each of the five suspended metal rods,
the five sounds of the black piano keys.
It makes a lullaby—
                    she loves the sane
intervals of the chimes, although in a recent dream
she drove the grand piano down the road
and found no place to park it.
After a life of music the musician said,
"But music, music has nothing to do with life."

The church had no steeple, not even
the usual gable pitched like praying hands.
Inside, bare whitewashed walls,
and in the white oak benches

no color there—
they all wore white or black,
long dresses, hats and beards,
as though any artifice were vile;

likewise no instruments:
not that the boxed piano was a sin
but the wish to play it,
which set one soul apart;

but the whole congregation
knew the songs—the gifted
and the tone-deaf equally—
those slow monophonic tunes

that seemed to rise in the church
the way the church had risen
in the clearing: plank by plank
and each plank true.

After Keats

1

If truth is not a thing apart from me,
then I don't want it.

2

       —Have you always told the truth?

I have always loved the truth.

Self-Portrait at LaGuardia

She completes the generic oval, a feathered
drape of hair across the brow, and then I know
my own round face will not emerge. In the strict row
of linked blue chairs, she's at my left,
paper cocked to let me see her hand
as it moves, as it shaves an inch of flesh
from below the chin, sharpens the cheekbones,
the piece of chalk adept at what can please.
And soon she guesses it pleases me
when she fiddles with the eyes,
adding lines and wrinkles, returning now
to turn the corners down and darken the pupils,
installing so much sadness and defeat I can almost think
her crayon found some other mission there,
beyond intent, beyond the vanity and commerce
all around us. But then she asks,
"Are you a weird shape, or is it me?"
tilts it so I see what she means, the mouth
too far to one side, right cheek
lumped and tired.
                        And what had I seen in her
to have pictured her descending on the East Side
into the streets, the park, the train, hungry for faces?

Now she lifts it toward me, what we've made.

The Harness

The lamp still lit in the studio,
the Master gone for dinner and his pipe,
and the boy in the upper branches of the tree,
taking his basket higher and higher—
Schumann repeating over and over the scales'
dull compulsory pattern—

                              the young Romantic,
coming to music late from studying law,
lived by the old idea,
Nature Emended, Nature-as-Machine: in his mind
he saw himself triumphant at the keys, his eager guests
dazzled by the fruit he had gathered.
But what he watched by the smoky lamp
were the hands of a clerk,
strapped in the strict corrective he devised,
pulley and weights, each finger made to lift alone
and thrust, like a dancer's leg, whole days of this—

All planets in alignment is a curse;
what's needed is resistance,
the gift struck against the circumstance;
what's needed is friction, as for a fire.
After the hand seized,
he turned to the blank page
and set the ruined thing to work again.

Thorn-Apple

They're walking in early evening, still light,
his head bent toward her but tilted slightly up,
the road a paved gully in these hills, on each side
a corridor of mullein and weeds, and beyond,
the damp unfolded bolts of patchy grass,
alfalfa blooming around the crippled trees,
the trees themselves cast on the slope
with symmetry enough to let her know
they once were planted there—
                                                    each detail
animates the flat abstracting mind he drifts inside,
its thick mist of dailiness and rue;
her task, endless and partial,
is willed attention: who had once been
subject and object, the artifact of desire.
Now she is the first one up the path—
the blindman's wife, brushing
a hand before her face as though
to open the beaded curtain of a door, her voice
sending back over her shoulder what she finds:
"gnarled"; then "dwarf"; then, "human,"
because the trees, seen from this distance,
seem contiguous but do not touch.

Variations: Thorn-Apple

Slender, cylindrical,
without a mark or seam,
almost wet against the rock;
wearing alternating bands
of black and yellow, and itself
coiled like a bracelet.
                    "Pretty, pretty,"
is what the baby said, reaching for it.

Muscular and fleet, he moves without thinking
among the shifting jerseys on the field.
In his wake the paler one,
through wave after wave of the enemy line,
presses the white ball forward: winded and earnest,
he has willed his body to this pitch
until the body is inside his mind
as the mind arranges pieces on the board—now
he cuts a wide angle and passes the ball
though he knows his friend will never give it back.
Ahead of him, always ahead of him:
this is the pattern
already set in their early victories,
one at the prow, one at the wheel.

Because it is a curse to be beautiful
and thus dismissed by other men,
the pretty man often wants to marry
mind, or grit, or great heart undistracted.
This is not the same as the lovely woman
who marries someone plain: she knows
the world's assessment has been wrong,
knows she is a fraud and proclaims it
with that mirror. The handsome man feels
no such scorn: yes, he is as gorgeous
as they say, but it's not a useful currency,
except with the plain woman who marries him
as one would pocket found-money or plant a rose.
But the plain man, the homely man, the man
hunched like a cricket or built like a jug,
who marries beauty and covets his own wife,
the man who prays at the altar of his wife,
the man who weeps when he has her, weeps when she's gone—
remember Menelaus, how he burned?

Sleek, blue, the jays are beautiful
until they speak. She used to say
that when they cry like that, a gargle

harsh as the rusted handle of a pump,
there'll soon be rain:
she could hear the liquid in their voices.

He can't remember much of what she said:
his ear is less retentive than his eye,
and when she spoke

he was busy watching her mouth
dimple and pout, her mouth
painted as he liked it.

These days he thinks of her infrequently—
when the jay calls, when the fox
shrieks in the field like a thing imperiled—

and yet with other women,
moths on a screen,
his eye will trigger something in his mind

like sound. *Siren* is the word
for what he hears, beauty's warning:
within its pleasures, all its urgencies.

Pretty face, pretty girl,
what was the camouflage that afternoon—
the way you stooped to hide your breasts?
the scabs you'd wheedled into your upper arm?
The others left to tour the reptile house;
inside the tent of net
we stood as still as trees to watch the birds.
On the woodchip path, scratching like chickens,
a toucan and a smaller cockatoo
were magnets for the eye, vivid and thus exotic.
Then I heard it: on a low-slung branch
the dove so near we could have touched it, throat
puffed like a bellows between the tiny head and fat butt—

Priam looking down from the city wall,
Echo near the pool, Charles Bovary,
Anna Karenina standing by the track,
or the one who survives, rescued from the bridge,
the poor selling fake flowers on the street,
and on the stage, the frozen prodigy
or the brilliant mind that stutters when it speaks,
the woman who sleeps with the snapshot of her dead child,
the daughter whose father cherishes his girl
like the deer whose head is mounted on the wall

⌣

—And if the self break out of the self?
It comes to the garden wall, kneels in the shrubs,
from there maps the featureless surround.

Two Trees

At first, for the man and woman,
everything was beautiful.
Which is to say there was no beauty,
since there was not its opposite, its absence.
Every tree was "pleasant to the sight,"
the cattle also, and every creeping thing.

But at the center, foreground of the painting,
God put two trees, different from the others.
One was shrubby, spreading near the ground
lithe branches, like a fountain,
studded with fruit and thorns.
When the woman saw
this tree was good for food
and a tree to be desired to make one wise,
she ate,
            and also saw
the other, even more to be desired,
tallest in the garden, its leaves
a deeper green than all the rest,
its boughs, shapely and proportionate,
hung with sweet fruit that never fell,
fruit that made the birds nesting there
graceful, brightly plumed and musical,
yet when they pecked it showed no scar.

To eat from both these trees was to be a god.
So God kept them from the second fruit,
and sent them into thistles and violent weather,

wearing the skins of lesser beasts—
let them garden dust and stony ground,
let them bear a child who was beautiful,
as they had been, and also bear a child
marked and hateful as they would become,
and bring these forth from the body's
stink and sorrow while the mind cried out
for that addictive tree it had tasted,
and for that other, crown still visible
over the wall.

The Box

Everyday the boy marks her progress:
at the round window, her round eye,
the bluebird that scrambled in and out
with grass, or moss, with string, hair, wool,
the innermost feathers of her breast. And if
he's spotted her in the bush or on the wing,
he lifts away the front wall of her house
with the same zeal that pulls the flap
of the mailbox: it's always news:
three small wet lumps of bird, so ugly, so tender,
those automatic, stretched-elastic mouths.

What happens in his kingdom while he sleeps?
In the still yard the old dog twitches,
the swing waits like a slingshot for its stone.
But close to daybreak, like a sturdy vine, something
muscles up the slender pole—
it sways with the weight
enough to startle the grown bird to a tree
where she watches the last long inches of that body
clear the hole. Now she circles and dives, flies
to the pin oak, flies to the fence, to the pine,
flies back—speech a child won't recognize
as he crosses the grass
to where the vivid parent stitches the air,
to where, caught like a rope by the knot in its neck,
the first hard lesson fills the quiet box—
bored but not impatient,
and a little sleepy.

The Innocents

Not as one might slip into a stream,
though it is a stream,
nor as we slide from sleep or into sleep,
but as the breath of a passing animal
unmoors a spore from the lacy frond
is the soul brought out of heaven.

It is another buoyancy.
With only the briefest fitfulness
the mote hangs in the vapor above the pond,
the crumb rides at the end of the supple line
on the skin of the river
until the slick fish swallows.

    One fish, two fish, how many of God's fish
    swam out of the sea?

    Muskrat, mud rat, does the toothed water rat
    still hunt in the sea?

    Night bird, nested bird, who drew the whistling bird
    so far from the sea?

    Red fox, brown fox, can any hungry silver fox
    remember the sea?

Soft Cloud Passing

1

Ice goes out of the pond as it came in—
from the edges toward the center:

large translucent pupil of an eye.

If the dream is a wish,
what does she wish for?

Soft cloud passing between us and the sun.

2

The plucked fields,
the bushes, spent and brittle,
the brown thatch on the forest floor
swoon beneath the gathered layers of gauze
before the earth is dragged once more into blossom.

And the woman at the window, watching the snow,
news of the child just now upon her—
she has the enviable rigor of the selfish,
light that seems so strong because withheld.
Already she cannot recall her former life.
She puts her face against the glass
as though listening.

Deer yarded up in the bog,
dogpack looking for deer.

3

The child is hot to her hand, less on his white
forehead beneath the damp foliage of hair
than in the crevices of thigh, belly, knee, dumpling-foot.
The telephone on the desk is a lump of coal.
She fans him with a magazine, she sponges
his limbs, her hands move up and down
as if ironing: this is how she prays,
without a sound, without closing her eyes.
When daylight was first sufficient to see the snow
falling, fine as sugar, it seemed an answer,
God chilling the world to save a child,
although she knows that isn't how it works.
Her husband naps in a chair;
doctor three blocks over, drugstore on the corner—
how often she walked past, pushing the stroller.
She lifts the baby closer to her heart.
The streets are clear, the sky clear, the sun
radiant and climbing:
the shelf of her breast will have to be the snow.
And so she holds him tighter, tighter,
believes she feels him cooling in her arms.

Woman Who Weeps

Up from the valley, ten children working the fields
and three in the ground, plus four who'd slipped like fish
from a faulty seine, she wept to the priest:
    Father, I saw the Virgin on a hill,
    she was a lion, lying on her side,
    grooming her blonde shoulders with her tongue.

Six months weeping as she hulled the corn,
gathered late fruit and milked the goats,
planted grain and watched the hillside blossom,
before she went to the bishop, kissed his ring.
    Father, I saw Our Lady in a tree,
    swaddled in black, she was a raven,
    on one leg, on one bent claw
    she hunched in the tree but she was the tree,
    charred trunk in a thicket of green.

After seven years of weeping,
not as other stunned old women weep,
she baked flat bread, washed the cooking stones,
cut a staff from a sapling by the road.
The Holy Father sat in a gilded chair:
    Father, I saw Christ's Mother in a stream,
    she was a rock, the water
    parted on either side of her,
    from one stream she made two—
    two tresses loosened across her collarbone—
    until the pouring water met at her breast
    and made a single stream again.

Then from the marketplace, from the busiest stall
she stole five ripened figs
and carried her weeping back to the countryside,
with a cloth sack, with a beggar's cup,
village to village and into the smoky huts,
her soul a well, an eye, an open door.

The Soothsayer

She looked at my hand as into a bowl of soup;
then simply held and stroked it. "Strong thumb,"
she said but without praise, meaning
able to make the most of what is given.
She had a local fame for finding things—
a ring, a cow—and with such patience
untangled the year's stalled stars
that I thought, watching her kindly farmer's face,
even if she could forecast disaster
she wouldn't; that's when she raised her chin and said,
"Some people think I never tell the bad parts,
but I do," and gave me what I came for:
"Two children, but only temporarily."
Short, aproned, grandmotherly,
she tried to clarify what she had seen,
but it didn't work, and then
she said that second-sight was more like listening,
that all I had to do was want it, her voice
was crooning, voice from a dream
in which we're swept downriver,
peril of my own volition—
what should I see?
My daughter on the green rug turning blue?
My newborn with a tube taped to his skull?
Ah, heart's-blood, twin chambers of my heart,
it was long ago, before I was your mother,
she placed that wrapped package in my palm.

Fish

Fish in a bowl, cat on the rug, a vase
of wild iris brought inside.
When I start to change the water for the fish
and scrub the tank—when I dip my net and the fish,
as usual, sprint from wall to wall
like something crazed—today
when I lift one out of the water

I see my child, hands tied at her side,
writhing and tossing in her transparent cage.
The nurse was coming toward her with a hose
to cut off the air and suck the mucus out.
And since what had to be cleaned
was in her throat and she could not speak,
her mouth closed and opened without a sound
on the **M**, the dark **ah**—

like a fish, mute and thrashing,
like a beached fish. But I didn't
think that then, watching: I think it now,
this fish in my net
and me thrown back ten years.

Variations: The Innocents

How far must the fruit fall from the tree?
When the youngest turned to his new wife,
I saw my mother stiffen into grief.
Although she'd always held herself aloof
from open weeping—it was her best gift—
nothing had more branches than her grief.
We wanted the stars, the sun through an open roof,
room away from the deep taproot—the self
stirs, wakes from the safe shadow, as if
childhood had been a fever! That one brief
season, we were the fruit and not the tree.

He wants the world to see him as a horse, charging;
we see him as a horse cut in stone,
knee-deep in water.

So he withdraws. On his knees
he ferries the children pleased to be this frightened,
across the dangerous shallows of the rug,

just as, when they were smaller,
he carried them in a pouch about his belly,
like the sea horse with its jeweled eye:

just as, long before they could be born,
he carried them in the small, thin sac.

Every seditious thought I ever thought
is in her head; and in her mouth
its best expression—
                                murderous,
murderous thoughts of those we love:
what other hell is this seductive, the self
self-justified, stopping its ears?

And where in nature is the paradigm,
except that first division of the cell?
No compassion encoded there,

but one of us must speak with its voice
as if the other were the animal
gnawing the caught paw free.

What can help my friend in his despair?
It is his great intelligence that appalls him. That,
and the broken trellis of his choices,
if the shaped vine
can be said to choose. And now the vine
is laid along the ground, now his life, planted
in the yard, has been flung forward,
no longer held to the side of the house
but only stitched here and there to the earth
by its own frail root hairs
as it disappears among the dense grasses, his mind
not merely a blossom on it but a melon:
yes, a melon ripening, and no one
to bring the knife, the clean white plate.

On the studio door, the tacked-up typed-up mottoes:
To see clearly is to understand; and,
Art cannot redeem what it does not love.
Inside, many large unfinished paintings;
at the center, "Parents, Drifting out to Sea,"
the small boat, the foolish rations, how gulls
dove and squabbled in their wake.
Of course she knew where all such journeys end.
And yet, there came the moment—
as if she looked away,
but she didn't look away—suddenly,
each had fallen over the bent horizon,
first one speck and then the other:
the one at the helm; the one
waving from the stern her soft scarf.

The cast bread stalls, drifts in a slow circle
like a boat whose one oar has been thrust down
to the sandy bottom. The surface stills.
The little boat bobs once; bobs again;
then a long shape takes it, slams it
into the granite bulkhead of the bridge
and there are fifty fish, a hundred fish
darkening the pond—carp come out of the silt,
a cubic yard of fish crowding the slick sides
of other fish, every size of gray torpedo
trying to sink the soggy loaf that is,
by now, in ruins, defeated by
the healthy fish that climb entirely
out of the water on the others' backs,
a loose pyramid of fish, white
bellies slung at the wall, three more
minutes of this until the bread is gone.
The mass of fish likewise breaks apart.
Each drifts away, except for one large carp—
shrewd, or stubborn, or perhaps only
hungrier than the others—
cruising the spot for wreckage—

When the deaf child came to school they tied his hands.
They meant to teach him speech, the common language.
They meant to cast him down into silence
    only a little while.
They showed him their teeth, their pink gymnastic tongues.
And raised him up with exaggerated praise
    if his face made the shapes their faces made,
    if he made his mouth a funnel for the sound
      and opened his throat to let the angel out.

His hands lay on his desk as though they were sick.
Like the two sick chimps he saw at the zoo.
One ran to the wire—knuckles swept the ground—
    rolling her lips under, exposing the gums.
The other was turned away from his audience,
    fingers and opposable thumbs
      stripping the leaves from a wand of the tree.
Perhaps it would be a tool; perhaps, a weapon.

On the coast of Chile, summer to our winter,
each day in any weather the people come
with notes, petitions, mantras, lines of the verse
to scrawl on the barricade around the house
Neruda lived and died in, where his ghost
came back as an eagle, as he said he would,
crashed through the picture window with its high
spectacular view of the sea and the cliffs, thrashed
the books and papers to the floor (some say
shat on them), and sat, wings closed, like the bronze
eidolon on a Roman consul's staff,
or like the consul, with his cloak and sword.

Herzenlied

Floodgates open upriver, the current
frothing beneath me like the dirty river
toward which he hurled himself
(as toward his drowned sister) and was hauled up,
I was crossing an iron bridge when I heard it,
his last great work, composed
mid-century a century ago,

the cello line as leisurely and sweet
as when I heard it first in the dark hall
where I sat with my life-mate, the two of us
two loons on a brackish water, for once
in concert, as they say, though one
was watching the face and one the fingers:

now, driving alone on the crooked road, I heard
the man who wrote what he could no longer play,
wrote pieces I had played when pressed, uncles
out on the stoop, aunts crammed in the front room
talking, *tutti, fortissimo,* outtalking
music that plumbed the new, the Grand Ideal:

and because he loved the secondary parts;
because he made the solo voice so often
yield to its companions—Heine and Goethe,
Chopin, Mendelssohn, and the young reverential Brahms,
a larva burrowing into his heart, his household—
because the will compels us and is blind,

I thought I heard,
                    as the sun, angled high,
struck the dun surface like an anvil,
the rest of his life foreshadowed—
after the Rhine, a cell—
so that the Androscoggin, wreathed
in foul yellow air from the paper mills,
became, for a moment, another river, and Schumann
not merely one of the souls ferried over
but the ferryman in the prow, easing us
with a last, passionate lie.

The Pond

Eight years. This week
he would have turned off asphalt at the gate,
crossed the cattleguard, straddled the ruts in the road,
forded broomstraw toward the stand of pines, flushing a dove,
and spent his birthday at the weedy pond.
Muddy, scummed, filling with fallen branches
and grasses that will thicken into marsh—

from the highway, you wouldn't know it's there,
this postcard of the Pleistocene. At century's end
what used to be done with the hands is done with machines,
freeing another brain:
This is the progress he had labored for,
trading the mule for a horse, the horse for a tractor,
finally trading frontage off the farm.
Even in his lifetime
he could hear, from his own porch,
suburban families in their yards.

Can unexpected death be seen as willed?
He'd cultivated everything he had.
He'd seen the hillside prosper.
He believed in an actual heaven.
There are two uncompromised sites left on his land:
half-acre of polished stones we put him in,
and the hole he dug himself,
a run-off pond, shallow, subversive,
where frogs feed on the minnows, snakes on the frogs.

The Letters

The drawer is full of letters. They rustle and sigh.
Sometimes, when he leaves the drawer ajar
their muffled conversation
leaks out like spices from a lifted lid.
At night he opens the drawer, stuffs in a letter—
they are not arranged
but flop and tumble like unmarried socks,
like the underwear he keeps in a neighboring drawer.
Blue ink: lined white paper: the writing on the paper
perpendicular to the lines but also prissy,
lacy as a young girl's underwear.
And some of the pages are themselves ajar, loosened, languid,
like odalisques, like figures in Matisse,
some lie on their sides with upturned signatures,
some are pleated like an unused fan.
Beside the bed, close enough to reach them in his sleep,
six months of letters squirreled home from school,
then plucked from the bag of unsatisfactory lunch,
or from the pocket of the laundered jeans,
or from the kitchen table where they'd dropped,
blossoms past ripening, from the stem.
Blue ink: lined white paper: familiar
as the letter waving in my mother's hand.

Gobelins

We came with the children up out of the Métro
thinking about the heroes we had seen
on the large dark canvases in the Louvre, how they knew
to look directly was to be turned to stone, or lost, or to lose
whatever fluttered near the periphery,
the way we know to watch the sun's eclipse
in a blackened mirror, as one flat disk
slides behind the other:

and thinking too of the driven ones
who'd painted Perseus, Eros and Psyche,
Zeus in his various rich disguise—
who had fixed the unfolding story into a still,
not lifelike but like memory—and since the centuries
jumbled in my mind in the grand museum,
I was thinking of Monet, his paintings grown
enormous, the edges of the objects less distinct
as his eyesight failed and Giverny
fell into composite and design.

We meant to get to Rue Mouffetard
before the farmers packed up and went home,
to the plank tables heaped with cherries and beans,
globed onions and pyramids of the little yellow plums
themselves a painting—and took the old route there
up Gobelins, broad avenue
changed but not changed much in twenty years.
Freed from the map, we showed the children
the tiny bright tabac, the public baths,

the borrowed flat we lived in, new to each other,
the famous factory behind the gate, its thick brocades
in which the maidens rise from a swirl of vines—

Tapestry is dumb, my son said, like
upholstery, and the four of us concluded on the spot
we were hungry, and stopped at the next café
on Avenue des Gobelins, whose weavers
always worked from behind the frame
where knots and stitches steadied the mind,
from time to time parting the warps with their fingers
and peering through, as through tall grass, at the shape
emerging, reversed, in the burnished shield.

Song and Story

The girl strapped in the bare mechanical crib
does not open her eyes, does not cry out.
The glottal tube is taped into her face;
bereft of sound, she seems so far away.
But a box on the stucco wall, wired to her chest,
televises the flutter of her heart—
news from the pit—her pulse rapid and shallow,
a rising line, except when her mother sings,
outside the bars: whenever her mother sings
the line steadies into a row of waves,
song of the sea, song of the scythe

        old woman by the well, picking up stones
        old woman by the well, picking up stones

When Orpheus, beating rhythm with a spear
against the deck of the armed ship, sang
to steady the oars, he borrowed an old measure:
broadax striking oak, oak singing back,
the churn, the pump, the shuttle sweeping the warp
like the waves against the shore they were pulling toward.
The men at the oars saw only the next man's back.
They were living a story—the story of desire,
the rising line of ships at war or trade.
If the sky's dark fabric was pierced by stars,
they didn't see them; if dolphins leapt from the water,
they didn't see them. Sweat beaded their backs
like heavy dew. But whether they came to triumph
or defeat, music ferried them out

and brought them back, taking the dead and wounded
back to the wave-licked, smooth initial shore,
song of the locust, song of the broom

      old woman in the field, binding wheat
      old woman by the fire, grinding corn

When Orpheus, braiding rushes by the stream,
devised a song for the overlords of hell
to break the hearts they didn't know they had,
he drew one from the olive grove—
the raven's hinged wings from tree to tree,
whole flocks of geese crossing the ruffled sky,
the sun's repeated arc, moon in its wake:
this wasn't the music of pain. Pain has no music,
pain is a story: it starts,
Eurydice was taken from the fields.
She did not sing—you cannot sing in hell—
but in that viscous dark she heard the song
flung like a rope into the crater of hell,
song of the sickle, song of the hive

      old woman by the cradle, stringing beads
      old woman by the cradle, stringing beads

The one who can sing sings to the one who can't,
who waits in the pit, like Procne among the slaves,
as the gods decide how all such stories end,
the story woven into the marriage gown,

or scratched with a stick in the dust around the well,
or written in blood in the box on the stucco wall—
look at the wall:
the song, rising and falling, sings in the heartbeat,
sings in the seasons, sings in the daily round—
even at night, deep in the murmuring wood—
listen—one bird, full-throated, calls to another,
little sister, frantic little sparrow under the eaves.

KYRIE

(1995)

For Dudley and Will

*Nothing else—no infection, no war, no famine—
has ever killed so many in as short a period.*

—ALFRED CROSBY,
America's Forgotten Pandemic: The Influenza of 1918

Prologue

After the first year, weeds and scrub;
after five, juniper and birch,
alders filling in among the briars;
ten more years, maples rise and thicken;
forty years, the birches crowded out,
a new world swarms on the floor of the hardwood forest.
And who can tell us where there was an orchard,
where a swing, where the smokehouse stood?

All ears, nose, tongue and gut,
dogs know if something's wrong;
chickens don't know a thing, their brains
are little more than optic nerve—
they think it's been a very short day
and settle in the pines, good night,
head under wing, near their cousins
but welded to a lower branch.

Dogs, all kinds of dogs—signals
are their job, they cock their heads,
their backs bristle, even house dogs
wake up and circle the wool rug.
Outside, the vacant yard: then,
within minutes something eats the sun.

Dear Mattie, You're sweet to write me every day.
The train was not so bad, I found a seat,
watched the landscape flatten until dark,
ate the lunch you packed, your good chess pie.
I've made a friend, a Carolina man
who looks like Emmett Cocke, same big grin,
square teeth. Curses hard but he can shoot.
Sergeant calls him Pug I don't know why.
It's hot here but we're not here for long.
Most all we do is march and shine our boots.
In the drills they keep us twenty feet apart
on account of sickness in the camp.
In case you think to send more pie, send two.
I'll try to bring you back some French perfume.

When does a childhood end? Mothers
sew a piece of money inside a sock,
fathers unfold the map of the world, and boys
go off to war—that's an end, whether
they come back wrapped in the flag or waving it.
Sister and I were what they kissed goodbye,
complicitous in the long dream left behind.
On one page, willful innocence,

                                    on the next
an army captain writing from the ward
with few details and much regret—a kindness
she wouldn't forgive, and wouldn't be reconciled
to her soldier lost, or me in my luck, or the petals
strewn on the grass, or the boys still on the playground
routing evil with their little sticks.

To be brought from the bright schoolyard into the house:
to stand by her bed like an animal stunned in the pen:
against the grid of the quilt, her hand seems
stitched to the cuff of its sleeve—although he wants
most urgently the hand to stroke his head,
although he thinks he could kneel down
that it would need to travel only inches
to brush like a breath his flushed cheek,
he doesn't stir: all his resolve,
all his resources go to watching her,
her mouth, her hair a pillow of blackened ferns—
he means to match her stillness bone for bone.
Nearby he hears the younger children cry,
and his aunts, like careless thieves, out in the kitchen.

This is the double bed where she'd been born,
bed of her mother's marriage and decline,
bed her sisters also ripened in,
bed that drew her husband to her side,
bed of her one child lost and five delivered,
bed indifferent to the many bodies,
bed around which all of them were gathered,
watery shapes in the shadows of the room,
and the bed frail abroad the violent ocean,
the frightened beasts so clumsy and pathetic,
heaving their wet breath against her neck,
she threw off the pile of quilts—white face like a moon—
and then entered straightway into heaven.

The temperament of an artist but no art.
Papa got a piano just for her,
she used him best, made all the sisters try.
We rode the mule to lessons, birds on a branch—
you know what it meant to have your own piano?

Next, guitar. Then painting in pastels—
she stitched herself a smock, sketched a cow
she tied to the fence by the fringe of its tail, braided
the tail the cow left hanging there. Unschooled
in dance, too scornful of embroidery,

she seized on marriage like a lump of clay.
A husband is not clay. Unhappiness
I think can sap your health. Though by those lights
there's no good reason why I've lived this long.

When it was time to move, he didn't move,
he lay athwart his mother. She pushed and pushed—
she'd had a stone before, she wanted a child.

Reaching in, I turned him like a calf.
Rob gave her a piece of kindling wood,
she bit right through. I turned him twice.

Her sisters were all in the house, her brother
home again on leave—
                              in the months to come
in the cities there would be families
reported their terminals and fled,
                                        volunteers
would have to hunt the dying door-to-door.

It started here with too many breech and stillborn,
women who looked fifty not thirty-two.
I marked it childbed fever in my log.

Nothing would do but that he dig her grave,
under the willow oak, on high ground
beside the little graves, and in the rain—
a hard rain, and wind

enough to tear a limb from the limber tree.
His talk was wild, his eyes were polished stone,
all of him bent laboring to breathe—
even iron bends—

his face ash by the time he came inside.
Within the hour the awful cough began,
gurgling between coughs, and the fever spiked,
as his wife's had done.

Before a new day rinsed the windowpane,
he had swooned. Was blue.

Dear Mattie, Pug says even a year of camp
would not help most of us so why not now.
Tomorrow we take a train to New York City,
board a freighter there. You know how the logs
are flushed through the long flume at Hodnetts' Mill,
the stream flooding the sluice, the cut pines
crowding and pushing and rushing, and then
the narrow chute opens onto the pond?
I'll feel like that, once we're out to sea
and seeing the world. I need to say
I've saved a bit, and you should also have
my grandpa's watch—tell Fan that I said so.
Keep busy, pray for me, go on with Life,
and put your mind to a wedding in the yard.

In my sister's dream about the war
the animals had clearly human expressions
of grief and dread, maybe they were people
wearing animal bodies, cows at the fence,
hens in their nests. The older dog implored her
at the door; out back, aeroplanes
crossing overhead, she found the young one
motionless on the grass, open-eyed,
left leg bitten off, the meat and muscles
stripped back neatly from the jagged bone.
For weeks I thought that was my fiancé,
the mailbox was a shrine, I bargained with
the little god inside—I didn't know
it was us she saw in the bloody trenches.

My father's cousin Rawley in the Service,
we got word, and I think a neighbor's infant,
that was common, my mother'd lost one too.

Then he went to town to join the war.
The sheriff hauled him home in an open rig:
spat on the street, been jailed a week or two.

She ran from the henhouse shrieking, shaking eggs
from the purse of her white apron to the ground.

Before I was born, he built a wide oak drainboard
in the kitchen, didn't just glue the boards,
screwed them down. Glue held, one split in two.

My mother was an angel out of heaven.
My father was a viper. I wished him dead,
then he was dead. But she was too.

My brothers had it, my sister, parceled out
among the relatives, I had it exiled
in the attic room. Each afternoon
Grandfather came to the top stair, said
"How's my chickadee," and left me sweet
cream still in the crank. I couldn't eat it
but I hugged the sweaty bucket, I put
the chilled metal paddle against my tongue,
I swam in the quarry, into a nest of ropes,
they wrapped my chest, they kissed the soles of my feet
but not with kisses. Another time: a man
stooped in the open door with her packed valise,
my mother smoothing on eight-button gloves,
handing me a tooth, a sprig of rue—

O God, Thou hast cast us off, Thou hast scattered us,
　　Thou hast been displeased, O turn to us again.
Thou hast made the earth to tremble; Thou hast broken it;
　　heal the breaches thereof; for it shaketh.
Thou hast showed Thy people hard things; Thou hast made us
　　to drink the wine of astonishment.

Surely He shall deliver us from the snare,
He shall cover us with His feathers, and under His wings,
　　We shall not be afraid for the arrow by day
　　nor for the pestilence that walketh in darkness.
A thousand shall fall at our side, ten thousand shall fall,
　　but it shall not come nigh us, no evil befall us,
Because He hath set His love upon us. . . .

　　　　　　　　　　　Here endeth the first lesson.

How can she be his mother—he had one of those
and knows she isn't it—odd, stiff,
negative of her sisters:
                          like large
possessive animals they are, grooming
the small inscrutable faces with their spit.

But here's the boy, culled from the loud clump,
and she can give him courtesy and work,
and since he seems to love to play outside

they work his mother's garden, grubbing out
the weeds and grass, the marginal and frail,
staking the strongest fruit up from the dirt.

Together they'll put by what they don't eat,
jars and jars of it—greens, reds, yellows
blanched in the steaming kitchen, vats of brine.

Hogs aren't pretty but they're smart,
and clean as you let them be—in a clean pen,
hogs are cleaner than your average cat:
they use their nose to push their shit aside.
And not lazy; if a hog
acts sick, you know it's sick.

As long as I've known hogs, I've known sick hogs,
especially in the fall, the cold and wet.
Before the weather goes, you slaughter hogs
unless you want to find them on their sides,
rheumy eyes, running snout.

It's simple enough arithmetic,
so don't you think the Kaiser knew?
Get one hog sick, you get them all.

Dear Mattie, Did you have the garden turned?
This morning early while I took my watch
I heard a wood sparrow—the song's the same
no matter what they call them over here—
remembered too when we were marching in,
the cottonwoods and sycamores and popples,
how fine they struck me coming from the ship
after so much empty flat gray sky,
on deck winds plowing up tremendous waves
and down below half the battalion ill.
Thirty-four we left behind in the sea
and more fell in the road, it's what took Pug.
But there's enough of us still and brave enough
to finish this quickly off and hurry home.

All day, one room: me, and the cherubim
with their wet kisses. Without quarantines,
who knew what was happening at home—
was someone put to bed, had someone died?
The paper said how dangerous, they coughed
and snuffed in their double desks, facing me—
they sneezed and spit on books we passed around
and on the boots I tied, retied, barely
out of school myself, Price at the front—
they smeared their lunch, they had no handkerchiefs,
no fresh water to wash my hands—when the youngest
started to cry, flushed and scared,
I just couldn't touch her, I let her cry.
Their teacher, and I let them cry.

Thought at first that grief had brought him down.
His wife dead, his own hand dug the grave
under a willow oak, in family ground—
he got home sick, was dead when morning came.

By week's end, his cousin who worked in town
was seized at once by fever and by chill,
left his office, walked back home at noon,
death ripening in him like a boil.

Soon it was a farmer in the field—
someone's brother, someone's father—
left the mule in its traces and went home.
Then the mason, the miller at his wheel,
from deep in the forest the hunter, the logger,
and the sun still up everywhere in the kingdom.

You wiped a fever-brow, you burned the cloth.
You scrubbed a sickroom floor, you burned the mop.
What wouldn't burn you boiled like applesauce
out beside the shed in the copper pot.
Apple, lightwood, linen, feather bed—
it was the smell of that time, that neighborhood.
All night the pyre smouldered in the yard.
Your job: to obliterate what had been soiled.

But the bitten heart no longer cares for risk.
The orthodox still passed from lip to lip
the blessed relic and the ritual cup.
To see in the pile the delicate pillowslip
she'd worked by hand, roses and bluets—
as if hope could be fed by giving up—

Snow heaped like a hat, square gray face,
the drift a shawl gathered at the neck—
a mailbox left unshoveled can be the sign,
a spirit crouching there beside the road—
I was at hand, I followed the doctor in:
Go ye therefore into the highways.
Renie had been the warning, months before
the universal pestilence and woe.
We'd had a late frost, a ruined spring,
a single jay was fretting in the bush,
quick blue smudge in the laden spikes of lilac:
it was an angel singing—don't you see:
it might as well have been a bush on fire.

A large lake, a little island in it.
Winter comes to the island and the ice
forms along the shore—when the first got sick
others came in to nurse them and it spread,
ice reaching out from the island into the lake.
Of course, there was another, larger shore—
Germany and Spain, New York, Atlanta,
ice also building *toward* the island.
By ice I'm thinking just those in the ground;
the sickness was more like brushfire in a clearing,
everyone beating the brush with coats and hands,
meanwhile the forest around us up in flames.
What was it like? I was small, I was sick,
I can't remember much—go study the graves.

Circuit rider, magic leather credential at my feet
with its little vials of morphine and digitalis,
I made my rounds four days at a stretch
out from the village, in and out of their houses
and in between, in sunlight, moonlight,
nodding on the hard plank seat of the buggy—
it didn't matter which turn the old horse took:
illness flourished everywhere in the county.
At Foxes' the farmhouse doors were barred by snow;
they prised a board from a window to let me in.
At the next, one adult already dead,
the other too sick to haul the body out—

deep in the lungs a cloudiness not clearing;
vertigo, nausea, slowed heart, thick green catarrh,
nosebleeds spewing blood across the room—
as if it had conscripted all disease.
Once, finding a jug of homemade corn
beneath the bed where a whole fevered family
lay head to foot in their own and the others' filth,
I took a draught and split the rest among them,
even the children—these the very children named for me,
who had pulled them into this world—
it was the fourth day and my bag was empty,
small black bag I carried like a Bible.

The barber, the teacher, the plumber, the preacher,
the man in a bowler, man in a cap,
the banker, the baker, the cabinet-maker,
the fireman, postman, clerk in the shop,

soldier and sailor, teamster and tailor,
man shoveling snow or sweeping his step,
carpenter, cobbler, liar, lawyer,
laid them down and never got up.

O, O, the world wouldn't stop—
the neighborhood grocer, the neighborhood cop
laid them down and never did rise.
And some of their children, and some of their wives,
fell into bed and never got up,
fell into bed and never got up.

Dear Mattie, Though you don't tell of troubles there,
meaning to buy me peace I would suppose,
dreadful word goes around, families perished
or scattered. I remind myself Pug's mother
died from having him and he thought orphans
saved themselves some time in the scheme of things—
won't a future happiness be ransomed
by present woe? Dear Mattie, it's you
I think of when I say my prayers, your face,
it's you I'll want when I get back from this
just like the night that I said Marry me
and you said Yes, and the moon came
from behind the cloud as I had wished it to,
and I kissed your mouth, and then your chestnut hair.

How we survived: we locked the doors
and let nobody in. Each night we sang.
Ate only bread in a bowl of buttermilk.
Boiled the drinking water from the well,
clipped our hair to the scalp, slept in steam.
Rubbed our chests with camphor, backs
with mustard, legs and thighs with fatback
and buried the rind. Since we had no lambs
I cut the cat's throat, Xed the door
and put the carcass out to draw the flies.
I raised an upstairs window and watched them go—
swollen, shiny, black, green-backed, green-eyed—
fleeing the house, taking the sickness with them.

Oh yes I used to pray. I prayed for the baby,
I prayed for my mortal soul as it contracted,
I prayed a gun would happen into my hand.
I prayed the way our nearest neighbors prayed,
head down, hands wrung, knees on the hard floor.
They all were sick and prayed to the Merciful Father
to send an angel, and my Henry came.
The least of these my brethren, Henry said.
Wherefore by my fruits, Henry said.
All of them survived—and do you think
they're still praying, thank you Lord for Henry?
She was so tiny, we kept her in a shoebox
on the cookstove, like a kitten.

What were they thinking—everyone we knew,
in school, in church, took me aside
to praise—to me—my sister, as if
I were another of her parents,
or else *they* were, that proud and fond:
aren't you lucky, isn't she gifted,
doesn't she look grand in her new blue suit?
I had a new suit cut from the same bolt,
quick mind, good heart—vivid blossoms
in other light—yes yes, she did, she was,
what were they thinking? Terrible,
to be the one who should have died.

Sweet are the songs of bitterness and blame,
against the stranger spitting on the street,
the neighbor's shared contaminated meal,
the rusted nail, the doctor come too late.

Sweet are the songs of envy and despair,
which count the healthy strangers that we meet
and mark the neighbors' illness mild and brief,
the birds that go on nesting, the brilliant air.

Sweet are the songs of wry exacted praise,
scraped from the grave, shaped in the torn throat
and sung at the helpful stranger on the train,
and at the neighbors misery brought near,
and at the waters parted at our feet,
and to the god who thought to keep us here.

He planned his own service, the pine box,
the open lid, which hymns, chapter and verse,
who would pray, how long, who'd carry him out.
He wrote it all down in a fair hand,
stroking the shawl around him in his chair,
and gave away his watch, his dog, his house.

Emmett said, he'd have lain down in the grave
except he needed us to tuck him in.

He shaved each day, put on his good wool pants
chosen for the cloth and a little loose
as they lowered in another son-in-law.
Sat by the door, hand-rolling cigarettes
three at a time, licking down both ends,
and wheezed and coughed and spit in a rusted can.

After I'd seen my children truly ill,
I had no need to dream that they were ill
nor in any other way imperiled—
no more babies pitching down the well,
no more watching from shore as my boy rolls
like a kicked stone from the raft, meanwhile
Kate with a handful of bees—

                    when I was a girl,
I practiced in the attic with my dolls,
but Del went out of right mind, his fingernails
turned blue, and Kate—no child should lie so still,
her small excitable body held enthralled. . . .
After that, in order to make it real
I dreamed them whole.

Dear Mat, For the red scarf I'm much obliged.
At first I couldn't wear it—bright colors
draw fire—but now I can. We took a shell
where three of us were washing out our socks
in a crater near my post. Good thing
the sock was off my foot since the foot's
all to pieces now—don't you fret,
it could have been my head, I've seen that here,
and then what use would be your pretty scarf?
The nurse bundles me up like an old man,
or a boy, and wheels me off the ward,
so many sick. But the Enemy suffers worse,
thanks to our gawdam guns as Pug would say.
Victory will come soon but without me.

The bride is in the parlor, dear confection.
Down on his knee at the edge of all that white,
her father puts a penny in her shoe.

Under the stiff organza and the sash,
the first cell of her first child slips
into the chamber with a little click.

The family next door was never struck
but we lost three—was that God's will? And which
were chosen for its purpose, us or them?

The Gospel says there is no us and them.
Science says there is no moral lesson.
The photo album says, who are these people?

After the paw withdraws, the world
hums again, making its golden honey.

Home a week, he woke thinking
he was back in France, under fire;
then thought the house on fire, the noise and light,
but that was from the fireworks and the torches
and on the square, a bonfire—everyone,
in nightclothes, emptied from their houses,
drawn toward a false dawn as from a cave—

oh there was dancing in the streets all right,
and singing—"Over There," "Yankee Doodle,"
"Mine Eyes Have Seen the Glory," I recall,
and "Camptown Races," who knows why—he plunged
into the crowd, tossed his crutch to the flames,
kissed delirious strangers on each side.

Say he lived through one war but not the other.

I told him not to move, they'd said *don't move*.
The weeks of fewer cases were a tease,

a winter thaw that froze back up worse
than before, backswing of a scythe, we filled

the gym, cots and pallets on the floor.
And many now in uniform—I could spot

who'd been gassed, their buttons were tarnished green—
and many of them were missing parts, like him.

Did I say the nurses were wearing masks?
My last day she put him next to me,

sweet little nurse but not enough of her
to go around she said *don't let him move.*

You tell me, was it prayer or luck kept
me from being that boy reaching for water?

I cried unto God with my voice . . . He gave ear unto me.
In the day of my trouble I sought the Lord;
   my sore ran in the night, and ceased not;
   my soul refused to be comforted.
I remembered God, and was troubled;
   I complained, and my spirit was overwhelmed.
I am so troubled I cannot speak.

Will the Lord cast off for ever? Is His mercy
   clean gone for ever? Does His promise fail
   for evermore? Has God forgot to be gracious?
   Has He in anger shut up His tender mercies?

Who is so great a God as our God?
   who has declared His strength among the people.

With no more coffins left, why not one wagon
plying all the shuttered neighborhoods,
calling for the dead, as they once did,
and let the living rest of us alone.
My father's pair of horses made the turn
at the big elm, onto the main road,
and we saw, strung out before us in the mud,
consecutive up the hill, links in a chain,
a caravan. Ahead of us in line:
three wrapped loaves. So I stared at the horse's head
between our mare's black ears, its brown ears framed
a gray, the gray a mule, until in the lead,
at the crest, was a child's toy, and a toy sled,
what lay in back shrunk to a cotterpin.

After they closed the schools the churches closed,
stacks like pulpwood filling the morgue,
but my cousin's husband's father "knew someone"
etcetera.
        Nobody else was there
but our own Parson Weems—to pray for us
and play the organ.
           Boy in a homemade box,
additional evergreens—rather grim
until the opening bars of "A Mighty Fortress"

flushed a bird from the pipes to agitate
around the nave. It's hard to cry if your head
is swiveled up,
         much less with bird manure
dropping "like the gentle rain"
on empty polished pews, plush carpet,
shut casket. Besides, I'd cried enough.

Who said the worst was past, who knew
such a thing? Someone writing history,
someone looking down on us
from the clouds. Down here, snow and wind:
cold blew through the clapboards,
our spring was frozen in the frozen ground.
Like the beasts in their holes,
no one stirred—if not sick
exhausted or afraid. In the village,
the doctor's own wife died in the night
of the nineteenth, 1919.
But it was true: at the window,
every afternoon, toward the horizon,
a little more light before the darkness fell.

Nothing fluttered, or sighed against her spine,
or coiled, recoiled in a fitful sleep,
fist in a sack, but her breasts knew
what her body made, and in her mind
she saw two legs, two arms, two plates of bone
where the damp tulle wings had been. Whatever it was,
she bled it out.

More snow fell,
into the deep ravine, the lesser gullies.
The doctor patted her arm: she was young, strong,
soon there would be another. But there wasn't:
just the one dream, the one scar.

No longer just a stream, not yet a pond,
the water slowed and deepened, banks eroded,
redwing blackbird roosting on a stalk,
sometimes that rippled vee plowing the surface.
Each clear day, she walked to the willow oak,
raked the anemic grass, tidied the mounds,
walked back down to the house by way of the creek.
If the beaver had put in a stick, she took it out.
If a storm had dropped a branch, she hauled it off.
When milder weather came, she tucked her skirts
at the waist and waded in, dislodging trash
the beaver would recover. Months of this.
Twice she sent for the neighbor to trap it or shoot it,
but each time Fan said Emmett don't you dare.

Once the world had had its fill of war,
in a secret wood, as the countryside lay stunned,
at the hour of the wolf and the vole, in a railroad car,
the generals met and put their weapons down.
Like spring it was, as word passed over all
the pocked and riven ground, and underground;
now the nations sat in a gilded hall,
dividing what they'd keep of what they'd won.

And so the armies could be done with war,
and soldiers trickled home to study peace.
But the old gardens grew a tough new weed,
and the old lives didn't fit as they had before,
and where there'd been the dream, a stranger's face,
and where there'd been the war, an empty sleeve.

To claim the War alone changed everything
can't be entirely right, too few of us
went over there.

            My mother used to phone—
the telephone was new, electric lights,
cars among the horses on the street—
my mother every morning when we woke
rang around to see who else had died.
She and Uncle Henry had a faith
deaf as well as blind, but most of us,
the orphans and the watchers and the stung—

at recess there was a favorite game: the chosen
died, in fits and twitches, while the other
stood by to cross the arms on the chest—that angels
might get a better grip—and to weep.

Maybe the soul *is* breath. The door shut,
the doctor, needed elsewhere, on his rounds,
the bereaved withdrawn, preoccupied with grief,
I pack each orifice with hemp, or gauze,
arrange the limbs, wash the flesh—at least
a last brief human attention,

                       not like

those weeks the train brought in big wicker
baskets we had to empty and return,
bodies often so blue we couldn't tell
who was Colored, who was White, which
holy or civil ground to send them to,
plots laid out by dates instead of names. . . .

Have you ever heard a dead man sigh?
A privilege, that conversation.

Around the house uneasy stillness falls.
The dog stiffens the ruff at her ears,
stands, looks to the backdoor, looks to the stairwell,
licks her master's shoe. What she hears

must be a pitch high on the Orphic scale,
a light disturbance in the air,
like flicks of an insect's wings or a reed's whistle
distant and brief: he barely stirs.

Out in the kitchen something seems to settle—
cloth on a dish, dust on a chair?
The animal whimpers now but doesn't growl:
this absence has a smell.
                              Poor master,
it's touched him too, that shift in molecules,
but all he feels is more of what's not there.

I had other children and they've all
had children too, I know I am
the luckiest of men—my wife, my sons—
but the tongue goes to where the tooth had been.

He was our first. The War, he said,
was the one important story of his time,
a crucible.
                Right after he got sick
they quarantined the post, we were on our way
to nurse him through—
                            our brightest boy
who used to ride his horse the length of the trestle,
across the steep ravine of Cherrystone,
he had such faith in the horse, in himself—

we stayed at a little inn, they gave us Tea,
served the English way, with clotted cream.

I always thought she ought to have an angel.
There's one I saw a picture of, smooth white,
the wings like bolts of silk, breasts like a girl's—
like hers—eyebrows, all of it. For years
I put away a little every year,
but her family was shamed by the bare grave,
and hadn't they blamed me for everything,
so now she has a cross. Crude, rigid, nothing
human in it, flat dead tree on the hill,
it's what you see for miles, it's all I see.
Symbol of hope, the priest said, clearing his throat,
and the rain came down and washed the formal flowers.
I guess he thinks that dusk is just like dawn.
I guess he had forgot about the nails.

If doubts have wintered over in your house,
they won't go out. The residue in the cupboard
means they've built a nest of your neglect
and fattened in it, and multiply, like mice.
Soft gray velvet scurry on the floor?
The rational cat licks a foot and looks away.
All dread passes—any harm they do
is mostly out of sight, and it's not just
your failure anyway:
                              a plausible God
is a God of rapture, if not the falcon
at least the small decorous ribbon snake
that slept in the hay against the northern wall.
But look: what drips like a limp Chinese moustache
at the lips of the cat coming up the cellar stairs?

My mother died, I was eight, I was sent away—
that has no meaning, just a shape,
the room I've lived in. That morning, end of May,

there'd been a frost so hard it looked like snow,
white on the green fields, the startled cows.
Spring in the fields, wild onion spikes the clover—

so bitter, even the butter ruined.
I've known some to dump it at the barn,
but if I bought a lamp that didn't burn

I wouldn't dump the oil, I'd soak the wick.
Eating a slice raw will do the work:
you notice nothing in the milk but milk.

He stands by the bed, he sits beside the bed,
he lays his unfledged body on the bed
where she had lain. If he'd had the right words
in his prayer, if he'd stayed awake
all night, if he'd been good, been wise, perhaps
he could have brought her back, the way she drew him
out of his dark moods, guitar in her lap,
her hair lace and shadow on her cheek—
in the hard-backed book propped open by the lamp
the shape-notes swarmed like minnows on the page,
she'd said their lives were scripted there.
Nearby someone feeds the treasonous baby.
She lied is the first verse of his new life.

To have inherited a child, angry
and grieving; to have opened her rusted heart
that first full inch; to feel it seize on the cold air
rushing in; and now to pretend his story,
lost in the deep thicket of the others,
is not hers: he stole again from the store,
she whipped him home and locked him in the barn,
he set the barn on fire and ran away.
How could that be her sister's boy, asleep
in the trundle bed, or ratcheting through the field—
he loved to be outside—from the porch she'd see
the top of his head, golden as the wheat,
parting the wheat, and then the wheat
closing up behind him without a seam.

Girls adore their teacher in third grade,
boys wait till they're grown. They send a card,
they visit now and again, wives in the car,
and I squint to find in the formed face
the face I knew, that little ghost. Time
isn't a straight line, it's a scummy pond
our minds fish in, and I might hook
Price alive instead of me
but not the two of us, in the dream we'd had—
that's been crowded out by the actual,
my husband, those borrowed children. After lunch
it's Once Upon a Time—my gift to them—
always the same few stories, can't change a word,
it eases them to know how they will end.

What I remember best is my cousin's crow.
He found it, fed it, splinted its damaged wing,
and it came when he whistled it down, ate from his hand,
said, like a slow child, what he had said.
Emmett never used a leash or cage;
for a year it hulked in the big pine by the door
or in the windmill's metal scaffold, descending
for apple, a little grain, a little show.

Once God gave out free will, I bet He was sorry.
So much had been invested in the bird,
the bird not understanding gratitude.
Well again, it turned up in the yard
from time to time, no longer smart or amusing,
no longer *his,* just another crow.

Dear Mattie, Wanting this right I'll write it down.
At the rally, I signed up for the War.
My father wanted that, and Fan was there
with Del and Kate and A. T. Cocke, Rob
and Renie and their children waving flags,
the Hodnetts and the Foxes next to them,
Dr. Gilmore Reynolds on his porch,
and Rawley a hero in his uniform.
Your uncle held the Bible for the oath,
everyone cheered—could you and your sister hear it
down at the school? It was the best birthday,
are you proud of me, we hadn't thought
to be married anyway before the fall,
I should be home to bring the harvest in

Why did you have to go back, go back
to that awful time, upstream, scavenging
the human wreckage, what happened or what we did
or failed to do? Why drag us back to the ditch?
Have you no regard for oblivion?

History is organic, a great tree,
along the starched corduroy of its bark
the healed scars, the seasonal losses
so asymmetrical, so common—
why should you set out to count?

Don't you people have sufficient woe?

Epilogue

The snow against the glass is full of sleet,
loud sheets of it, lined on a strict diagonal,
a scrim between the farmhouse and the hill.

Marking the blurred horizon, five stiff trees,
windbreak—the residue as woods were pared away—
extended east and west by stone walls made

from what the earth cast up and didn't need.
Summer, under dumb clouds still benign, maternal,
as the narrow local stream rushed toward salt,

the drayhorse grazed where open field had been,
knee-deep in thistles, milkweed, fireweed, Queen Anne's lace,
his back a sprung hammock withers to tail,

his gut slung low and parallel, his sex,
unloosed from its suede holster, dimpled as crepe. Now
every stalk in the field is beaten down.

Such is the world our world is nestled in.
And what if the horse were installed in the barn with a bucket of oats?
Shush, says winter, blown against the window.

Author's Note

In March 1918, what the Germans would call "Flanders Fever" was first recorded at Camp Funston, Kansas; in April, disabled ninety recruits a day at Fort Devins; in May, struck 90 percent of the American forces at Dunkirk; by June, had infected eight million Spaniards; July, spread widely throughout India; August, sprouted in China and returned to New York on board a Norwegian ship; September, reached eighty-five thousand civilian cases in Massachusetts alone; on one October day, claimed seven hundred recorded deaths in Philadelphia; in November, subsided long enough for the repeal of laws that forbade shaking hands (Arizona) or required masks on public transport (San Francisco); then reemerged, more virulent and often among the same populations, as the troops came home. By March 1919, "Spanish" influenza had killed, by conservative estimate, more than twenty-five million worldwide.

Most of the victims were neither old nor very young nor particularly frail: the virus favored young adults, and the normal U curve of mortality figures warped into a Dutch girl's pointed hat. Once past the usual childhood diseases, the body redeploys its defense against more localized dangers, such as broken bones or wounds, for which the best response is inflammation: flooding the site with antibodies, white cells. This time, the infection was generalized—the entire interior surface of the lungs. On autopsy, normally delicate lung tissue was dense and sodden, the lungs two blue sacks of fluid. The victims drowned.

The U.S. toll was half a million dead: as many servicemen killed by influenza as in combat, and ten times that many civilians.[1] The figure does not include stillborns and women lost in childbirth, numbers elevated in the early months, nor the increase in deaths from pneumonia

---

[1] Current estimates are now commonly set at 675,000 U.S. deaths.

and tuberculosis during the epidemic period, nor those in whom the virus exacerbated a previous condition such as heart disease or pleurisy.

In one year, one quarter of the total U.S. population contracted influenza; one out of five never recovered. Nevertheless, the national memory bears little trace. There are a few notable records in our imaginative literature: Katherine Anne Porter's *Pale Horse, Pale Rider*; Willa Cather's *One of Ours*; Horton Foote's *Home Cycle*; and William Maxwell's *They Came Like Swallows*. A well-researched account is available from Alfred Crosby, *America's Forgotten Pandemic: The Influenza of 1918* (Cambridge University Press, 1989), from which the statistics cited here have been taken.

SHADOW OF HEAVEN

(2002)

For Joan

. . . though what if Earth
Be but the shadow of Heaven, and things therein
Each to other like, more than on Earth is thought?

—*Paradise Lost*

Winter Field

Largesse

Aix-en-Provence

Banging the blue shutters—night-rain;
and a deep gash opened in the yard.
By noon, the usual unstinting sun
but also wind, the olive trees gone silver,
inside out, and the slender cypresses,
like women in fringed shawls, hugging themselves,
and over the rosemary hedge the pocked fig
giving its purple scrota to the ground.

What was it had made me sad? At the market,
stall after noisy stall, melons, olives,
more fresh herbs than I could name, tomatoes
still stitched to the cut vine, the soft
transparent squid shelved on ice; also,
hanging there beside the garlic braids,
meek as the sausages: plucked fowl with feet.

Under a goose-wing, I had a violent dream.
I was carrying a baby and was blind,
or blinded on and off, the ledge I walked
blanking out long minutes at a time.
He'd flung a confident arm around my neck.
A spidery crack traversed his china skull.
Then it was not a ledge but a bridge, like a tongue.

From the window over my desk, I could look down
at the rain-ruined nest the *sangliers*
had scrabbled in the thyme, or up, to the bald

mountain in all the paintings. I looked up.
That's where one looks in the grip of a dream.

Apple Tree

No choice for the apple tree.
And after the surgeon's chainsaw,
from one stubborn root

two plumes of tree now leaf
and even blossom, sky's
cool blue between them,

whereas on my left hand
not a single lifeline
but three deep equal

channels—
          O my soul,
it is not a small thing,
to have made from three

this one, this one life.

Winter Field

The winter field is not
the field of summer lost in snow: it is
another thing, a different thing.

"We shouted, we shook you," you tell me,
but there was no sound, no face, no fear, only
oblivion—why shouldn't it be so?

After they'd pierced a vein and fished me up,
after they'd reeled me back they packed me under
blanket on top of blanket, I trembled so.

The summer field, sun-fed, mutable,
has its many tasks; the winter field
becomes its adjective.
                    For those hours
I was some other thing, and my body,
which you have long loved well,
did not love you.

The Others

Our two children grown, now
is when I think
of the others:
           two more times

the macrocephalic sperm battered
its blunt cell forward, rash
leap to the viscous egg—

                  marriage
from our marriage, earth and fire—
and what then,
           in the open

synapse from God's finger
to Adam's hand?
           The soul
sent back:

        our lucky
or unlucky lost, of whom
we never speak.

Practice

To weep unbidden, to wake
at night in order to weep, to wait
for the whisker on the face of the clock
to twitch again, moving
the dumb day forward—

is this merely practice?
Some believe in heaven,
some in rest. *We'll float,*
you said. *Afterward*
we'll float between two worlds—

five bronze beetles
stacked like spoons in one
peony blossom, drugged by lust:
if I came back as a bird
I'd remember that—

until everyone we love
is safe is what you said.

Himalaya

Branches: wings: we sheltered in thick fir trees.
The cliff-face, as we'd asked, had furnished trees.

When your mother died, I dreamed the wild mountain
of the grave, its myrrh and milk, fur and fleece.

I know what my soul saw: the sky like silk
pulled through a ring, a flock of wind-slurred trees.

Those feathery evergreens were blue—didn't you
wear blue for luck at all her surgeries?

Calm came into the dream, unburdened as snow.
It sugared the rocks, the rock-encircled trees.

You had no need to dream her back: your many
kisses were locks against death's burglaries.

Regret came into the dream thankless as snow.
It floured God's black beard, it furred the trees.

There was no pile of stones, laid one by one
to mark the leaden anniversaries.

No beasts, no birds—snow fine as smoke, and the only
quickened shapes, behind that curtain, were trees.

Years past, a soul slipped by the stone I was.
On the windowpane, frost's rucked embroideries.

Root and branch: the year of fasting ends.
Outside: veiled sun, snow's layered silks, blurred trees.

Whose ghost is it, Shahid, feeds my grief-dream?
Whose loss, whose task, whose darkened nursery?

Lesson

Whenever my mother, who taught
small children forty years,
asked a question, she
already knew the answer.
"Would you like to" meant
you would. "Shall we" was
another, and "Don't you think."
As in, "Don't you think
it's time you cut your hair."

So when, in the bare room,
in the strict bed, she said
"You want to see?" her hands
were busy at her neckline,
untying the robe, not looking
down at it, stitches
bristling where the breast
had been, but straight at me.

I did what I always did:
not weep—she never wept—
and made my face a freshly
white-washed wall: let her
write, again, whatever
she wanted there.

High Winds Flare Up and the Old House Shudders

The dead should just shut up. Already
they've ruined the new-plowed field:
it looks like a grave. Adjacent pine-woods,
another set of walls: in that dark room
a birch, too young to have a waist,
practices sway and bend, slope and give.
And the bee at vertical rest on the outside pane,
belly facing in, one jointed limb crooked
to its mouth, the mouth at work—
my lost friend, of course, who lifelong
chewed his cuticles to the quick. Likewise
Jane who calls from her closet of walnut and silk
for her widower to stroke her breasts, her feet,
although she has no breasts, she has no feet,
exacting pity in their big white bed.
The dead themselves are pitiless—
they keen and thrash, or they lodge
in your throat like a stone, or they descend
as spring snow, as late light, as light-struck dust
rises and descends—frantic for more, more of this earth,
more of its flesh, more death, oh yes, and a few more
thousand last vast blue cloud-blemished skies.

The Garden, Spring, The Hawk

from Baton Rouge, to my sister in Virginia

1

Like a struck match: redbird, riding the wet
knuckle of the longest limb of the leafless water oak,
pitching glissandi over the myrtle trees.
The yellow cat, one paw leveraged out of the soggy grass, then another,
has nothing to do with this: too slow, too old.
Nor the night-stunned snakes under the log, a cluster of commas;
nor the cloistered vole, the wasp, the translucent lizard,
the spider's swaddle of gauze, waiting to quicken.
This hour belongs to the birds—where I am,
single ripe berry on the bush; where you are,
Cooper's hawk, on the rail fence, dressing her feathers;
and the indistinct domestics at their chores.

2

While the prodigal husband is still asleep,
and the half-grown child, also sleeping, breathes in and out
as if that were the dullest task—while the migraine
loosens its fist and the pulse slows, one
overeager chamber of the heart and one reluctant
pumping together, lifting the blood and its boats
across the locks,
                    is it possible yet to sit
at the broad window, hands around a cup,
the furnace in a modest hum, and make your mind
the streaked, sweaty pane a rag rubs clear?
Tree: fence: frogpond the size of a tire: residual moon:
each a weight to hold the skull-flap down.

3

The very air voluptuous and droll,
sometimes wrung into mist or vertical rain, Tuesday
breezes of shifting magnitudes, diaphanous cloud,
by Wednesday afternoon unsullied sun
but not hot—the season at this latitude
seems coy,

        seems feminine, I nearly said,
a woman napping in a frothy gown, and credit
thinking it

        not to having been away so long,
or the multitude of songbirds, courting and throbbing,
or the slutty blossoming of shrubs, but coming back
at all:

        the country of one's origin
is always *she*, the ground beneath the plow,

4

and the Deep South a clearer paradigm
than where you live beside the northern gate:
or Carolina where I went to school among magnolias,
back row, far left, one more blank white face:

or the first hill at the junction of woods and field,
functional garden, random flowers unsolicited,
and beyond the redbrick house, houses we built
below the pines in the soft trash of the forest floor—
days, weeks, we colonized a wilderness; it needed that *we,*

and closed to both of us when you were twelve, thirteen.
Time to be groomed for the breathless hunt-and-run,
purse and title at the finish line.

5

As if I were the moss, D. said, electric
and dismayed. House behind us scaffolded and draped
for surgery, she was showing me those hanks of woeful hair
harvested from live oaks down the street and rehung here;
it lives on air, like the gray Confederate ghosts
she sleeps among. Long-married, transplant, more guest
than host, she has a forced-resilience look (like my friend C.,
divorced last year, her heart prised like a root
from its tight pocket).
                         Scissors and trowel: saw and chisel:
D. hired someone to help her stay, to knock away a wall
and put in glass. Like yours: window over the table,
row of doors to bring the outside in.

6

A back paw lifts: *adagio:* unlike
Thursday's cat harassing squirrels, untiringly,
that sallied forth from a clipped hibiscus, motoring
into open lawn where the hungry and the anxious
gathered food—hurry, hurry, they saw it coming on,
then leapt to a tree. After a long pause, the peril
hustled a straight line back to wait by the hedge.
Up and down the tree the squirrels flickered.
One by one they hazarded the ground.
Like criminals they angled toward the bread, nonchalant—
but spastic, too, their rigid compact bodies
ratcheting toward the source, the tree, the cat.

7

Soft, sweet, fetching, idle, pliable—whose
ideal was that? And how should it fit a childhood
reaching under a chicken for an egg? Or grown sisters, come
with gardens on their heads, who, at the sink, uncorseted,
let loose high-pitched complaint and low burlesque
as they itemized the Women's Fellowship, assaying
pew by pew the match that each had made.

Took me years to like that company. Meanwhile,
little pitcher with brains, I could see the men
leaning against the Packard in the yard, smoking,
toeing the hard red dirt, analyzing crops and cash,
or politics and war, or—or what? The world.

8

The slim successive cars like vertebrae
trailing the primitive skull, the train pulls forward,
past other trains and disconnected engines, Janus-faced;
negotiates the network of spurs and switches,
a thicket of poles and wires, sheer brick canyons,
signal-flags of laundry; passes the cotton mill's windows'
blind blue grid, and picks up speed downhill

as the late-model coupe turns left at the edge of town.
Windows open. Maps unpleated across the dash.
Something loud, popular and brisk, on the radio.

Now solve for x: how long, midday, they'll travel
neck and neck beside the broadening river. . . .

9

Against the brown field, bare trees, the hawk
swivels her head: becomes a bird. Cousin to eagle and kite,
marked like the smaller male she mates for life,
all that's vivid kept to the underside,

she doesn't touch the bread, the scraps of meat
you leave for the crows—it's mistakes she's after,
reckless mole, fledgling in the grass. The kitten
stays inside, hare in its hole. And you:
you've also learned to be good at holding still.

Why does a thing so fierce need camouflage?
Cooper's hawk, chicken hawk—you've seen her fly:
short wing-beats, and then the long glide.

10

Like an unsheathed falcon to the falconer
you *flew,* at eighteen, to his outstretched arm.
Restricted, addictive plural:
                                        and with it, your one
vocation. Why so eager for received idea?
This was not an absence of ambition but the heart thrown
like a rubbed coin. . . .

                        Harder now to wish, harder to choose,
something in you drained off, or worn away,
and not yet, in its place, a new resolve—

you said so, late last fall, under the dead
limbs of the largest dogwood in the yard:
I can't even imagine a different life.

And spaded in another dozen bulbs.

11

My beautiful capable daughter, far from home
where rocks outnumber blossoms, had this dream:

I'd planted the steep hillside behind the house,
mostly vegetables, and they were huge: my secret
was salt, in which the bell peppers thrived and fruited,
and lush tomatoes, flowers on the barn's south side,
the path down through them littered with purple roses
(only the clenched, introverted heads), I'd put them there,
purple her favorite so I knew she'd follow
the bend in the brook to the level field which was—
I'd planted this too—a broad expanse of white lace,
web of froth and steel: wedding gown.

12

Again and again the low-slung campus cat
charged out and back entirely purposeful:
that is, mechanical: in fact, remote-controlled
by a pleasant, detached young man behind the hedge,
studying Caution versus Appetite.
Clipboard, stopwatch, food, known patch of grass—
for the foragers, a closed set: he was measuring
how near his subjects let the danger come
before they bolted for the tree. Although by then
I could see it wasn't a very plausible cat,
remnants of shag glued to a model car,
it was hard to feel superior to the squirrels.

13

The cardinal sings and sings: hunter's horn;
then, artillery. The round red door to its heart
is always open. And now the same song
from down the street, this time a mockingbird,
which, like the emperor's toy, can do it better.

How many generations did it take to cultivate, in us,
the marriage gene? Or, if we simply learned our lessons well,
didn't you see it, smell it, in that air:
to loathe change is to loathe life—

Nevermind.
What you want from me is only an ear. Meanwhile,
the carpenter has come in his rusted truck
(Echo also does this bird quite well).

14

Once, there was a king with two daughters.
The older girl of course would take the throne.
And so it was left to the other to be clever.

Lead lute for the Young and Foolish Virgins,
she rode her great blue ox across the moat;
having a thorn in its hoof, it *needed* a friend.

She underwent the seven grueling labors.
She wrote a symphony. She wrote checks home.
Next, a sweet boy's rescue from the tower.

She cut his hair, he baked her bread, and soon
they were lumbering magnolias coast to coast—
it's that spilt seed strewn out across the heavens.

15

In the grass a beetle takes a quarter-turn;
in a week a window where there'd been a wall.
My hosts, plural and solicitous, apologize for winter's
monochrome, despite the fluent azalea, hibiscus, camellia—
whole trees of that soft fabric—aggressive bird:
one hundred shades of red. And basting the yard's edge
like stitches for a hem, like string at the mouth of a purse,
like a threading pulse, the cat prowls half-blind
among the shrubs. The student, asked if he had named
his cat, answered fast and earnest: "Oh no.
This is science." Intending, perhaps, like the exile,
to keep a little distance from what we are.

The Art of Distance

1

Wrinkle coming toward me in the grass—no,
fatter than that, rickrack, or the scallops a ruffle makes,
down to about the fourteenth vertebra. The rest of it: rod
instead of a coil.
                          So I'd been wrong the afternoon before
when the dog, curious, eager to play and bored with me
as I harvested the edge of the raspberry thicket,
stalked it from the back stoop to the lip
of the bank and grabbed the tip
in her mouth and tossed it—
sudden vertical shudder
shoulder-level—
                          wrong
to read survival in its cursive
spiraling back to the cellar window-well
where it had gathered field mice like a cat.
And now, if it meant to be heading for the brook,
it veered off-course, its blunt head raised
like a swimmer's in distress.
                          The functioning part
gave out just short of me, inside the shade
but not the bush; the damaged part,
two fingers thick, was torqued
pale belly up, sunstruck.
I left it where it was,
took the dog in, and for hours
watched, from the kitchen window, what seemed
a peeled stick, the supple upper body that had dragged it
now pointed away and occluded by the shade,

the uncut grass.
                    My strict father
would have been appalled: not to dispatch
a uselessly suffering thing made me the same, he'd say,
as the man who, seeing a toad,
catatonic Buddha in its niche, wedged
within the vise of a snake's efficient mouth
clamped open for, then closing slowly down and over it,
bludgeoned them both with the flat side of a hoe.

For once I will accept my father's judgment.
But this had been my yard, my snake, old enemy
resident at the back side of the house. For hours,
the pent dog panting and begging, I watched
from the window, as from a tower wall,
until it vanished: reluctant arrow
aimed at where the berries
ripened and fell.

2

My father was an earth-sign and a stoic,
an eldest child, a steward, who took dominion
over the given world—at least, it seemed,
his hundred acres of it, pets we ate,
rabbits minced in the combine, inchling moths
torched in the crotch of the tree to save the peaches.
Scorned excess and complaint. Importuned,
said *no, not, can't, never will.*
                                What didn't fit
was seeing him cry. He'd stand alone in the field
like a rogue pine that had escaped the scythe,
as he would stand beside the family graves,
a short important distance from the car
where we were hushed until the white flag
had been unpocketed, and he jangled his keys
and got back in, not ever looking at us,

not looking at the brisk instructive face
my mother used on clerks, on amputees.
This all happened long before my mother,
in charge of cheerfulness and world morale,
had lost a body-part and given up—
so it was never in response to her,
the way he wept, or equally the way

he moved through life, one hoof after another:
a sentimental man is singular,
still the boy whose mother's gone away.
The last full day of our last ritual visit—

he'd taken a turn already into the field—
what set him off was hearing the neighbor's gun.
She merely wanted the turtle out of her beans;

he hauled the carcass home, two feet wide,
a rock from the creek, and also elderly
if the shell's whorls correspond to xylem and phloem,
rings we'd count on the cut trunk of a tree.
"Tastes like chicken," he said, gathering
the saw, the maul, chisel, pliers, hatchet
he'd need to unhouse the body and chop it up.

No one wanted to help, or even watch,
except the child intent on the row of knives,
and the child changing her mind with a webbed foot's wave—
dinner was not quite dead—but shudders and tears
were weakness and wouldn't work, jokes wouldn't work
on temper alchemized from noun into verb
as my father pried the armored plates apart,

pale and sweating and silent. And never did he,
sun long gone down, once quit the bloody porch,
the bowl of the upper shell in shards, the entrails
bejeweled with flies, the beaked head, feet and tail
cast off into wet grass, until, at the screen,
holding a platter of meat, he might have been
the Queen's woodsman bringing back the heart.

I heated the oil until it spit at me,
dredged the pieces in flour as I would chicken,
flung them chunk by chunk into the pan.
When chewed undefeated lumps ringed even *his* dish,
he said I'd done the best I knew, not
naming the skill: deflecting sorrow and terror
into a steady fierceness, and aiming *that*.

3

They shaved the torso from behind the nape, across the shoulder
　　to the center chest, taking away exactly the noble ruff
　　　　and adjacent sable winter-thickened fur,

　　making, when she crouches at my feet, the joint and sinew
　　　　discernible under the startled skin,
　　　　　　as in those close-up photos from the Veldt,
　　　　　　as if she were hunched above a slack gazelle

(but when she's sleeping on her side, her neck, extended,
　　might be the slack gazelle's).

Fifty-seven stitches track from the spine,
　　inside the sheltering ridge of the collarbone,
　　　　down to where the trachea enters lung,
　　their puckered, punctuated seam gathering
　　　　what something split apart, some creature
　　　　　　cornered in the woods or field,

no trophy, no raw meat except her own, no carcass
　　pinioned now beneath her paws,
　　　　　　　　only the wretched quilt,

　　torn and stained—

an obedient, courteous dog, she is abashed to pee indoors,
　　she doesn't squat, she stands with her head low,
　　　　like a whipped horse, as the gush puddles the floor—

and even though (or because) mostly when I touch her it is
    to apply the many therapies prescribed, pills
        down her throat, hot compress on the draining wound,
    or to smooth the pallet of her lying-in,

she neither whimpers loudly nor draws back:

therefore, she seems not only dutiful
    but grateful, too, as though the touch conveyed
        a recognition; a bond
            if not of pain, indignity;
        compassion not for another but for oneself.

    Which makes my hand enact a tenderness.
Like the rough warm tongue that licks the weak one clean.

4

When you saw your father last, he was tied into a chair
with a soft sash: the nurses had parked him, nearly
weightless, near the window, in sunlight: the shook
filaments of fine white hair repelled

every bead of light as his tremorous head drooped on its stalk—
the whole stalk drooped, curving down and in, the chin
sank toward the concave chest, the arms were veined
sticks from the sleeves of the gown like a sack,

but his hands, delicate, unlined, *deliberate,* were reaching
forward as a small child might reach to stroke the warm
bright beam that struck his knees.
                                    "Still a doc,"
the charge-nurse said behind you at the door,

"still wants to diagnose." Said: the knees sometimes show
how close death is. A puffiness? Or granulated skin?
You didn't ask, seeing the focused will he lived by,
the avid mind, take its scientific measure,

the tips of the fingers glossing both kneecaps, comparing
each to each? Or, to the many patients in his head?
The rest of the body barely moved, except its slow
declension, the labored breaths so slow

and far apart: as though to practice for the long deep dive
the great sea-creatures make, only matched in humans
by the held moments when its brain shuts down
in order that the infant be delivered.

5

After lunch, on the side porch,
the uncinched wooden leg in a muddy boot
stood by the edge of the bed. Freed from the second boot:
a full-length human leg, denim on white chenille. The other
stopped at a blunt substantial thigh. Its puckered stump,
facing me, looked like a face, or a fist.
I looked at it hard.

Four hands, three legs and half
a brain, my uncle said: what my grandmother
salvaged from the war—her brother's wounded sons,
sullen Ed with his limp, Grover hunched and simpering.
They worked the fields and in the barn, ate in her kitchen,
hair slick from washing up, like the hired hands.
When she said grace,

my grandmother said it standing,
bandaging her hand in her apron skirt
to lift the cast-iron skillet out of its round hole
to the square table of men. Burn herself up, her daughters said,
on Sundays, visiting like me, and scolding my uncle,
but still she fed with her fingers the squat stove,
and her grown wards

chopped the wood and hauled it,
pumped water, hauled it, cut hay, hauled it, hauled
the pig and cow and chicken shit and stirred the flies.
You keep out of the barn, my uncle said, after he'd found me
rapt by what they'd found: thick braid hung from a beam—

two blacksnakes writhing there like a hot wire,
a lit fuse.

What else do you need to know?
That my uncle, who was the baby, who went to war
and came home whole, who had no children, had no brothers,
thereby got the farm, would sell the farm—my uncle brought home,
for Grover, a puppy that liked to sleep in my grandmother's lap
and lick her plate, dirty little dog
her daughters said;

and a slick red racing bike,
which was not, with its manual brakes, the joke you think:
Ed stretched his crutch on the rack of the handlebars, slued
the stiff leg out and pumped the other, his sly pleasure breaking
through perfected scorn, cruising the porch where I sat
hulling peas in a china bowl—sometimes
the world looks back.

6

The enormous world shimmering—
    then, in the magic glass, some of it,
        guessed at, came clear.

Whereas my friend "in nature"
    takes his glasses off so he
        "can think." When he says

he thinks with his body—body
    grown substantial over the years,
        as has his thought—

I don't know what he means; or,
    if I do, I think thinking is not
        the body's job,

that the body gets in the way.
    Our friendship feeds on argument.
        Each of us

has one prominent eye:
    his the one on the right, for the left
        side of the brain,

language and logic; but mine—
    wide and unforgiving—mine
        is the one on the left,

enlarged by superstition
    and music, like my father's more
        myopic eye.

Detachment is my friend's
    discovery, what he commends
        against despair.

And though my father claimed
    I never listen, of course I do:
        after all, who else

but the blind will lead the blind?
    And the years bring their own correction:
        to see a thing

one has to push it away.

7

What art, like money, does is dig things up,
so that each tree and bush has its plateau—
tufts of frond in palms five stories high;
the spare flamboyant tree that seeds in pods,
its bunched florets; frangipani trees
to sweeten the air, clusters of white blossoms
with yellow throats; the mangrove trees, from whose
dense canopies descend the branch-like roots,
serpentine; and close to the ground, hedges
of bougainvillea, odorless, origami,
sometimes two colors on a single branch—
all rescued from the wet interior,
its undivided green, its bamboo swamps,
its breadfruit, mango, cocoa, guava, plum,
its forests of nutmeg trees, of almond trees—

Nobody needs be hungry here, excepting
what they wants is meat, Carlton said
when you remarked an isolated goat,
skeletal, among papaya trees.
Carlton's Tours are in his Chevrolet
(tan '68 sedan, original clutch),
and Carlton, wearing a tie, means to please,
courtly, bluffing when he doesn't know,
although he knows the flora, and where to find
abandoned factories that once made rum,
and overgrown plantations, and also where
the aborigines last took their stand:
on a bare cliff, so that, having lost again,
they could, and did, fling themselves to the sea.

One needs, it seems, sufficient irony:
to see oneself and the island as from the clouds:
a speck on the back of a gecko turning brown
these weeks before the rains, as if to hide
from the gray square-headed bird, its needle-nose,
its white chest and belly and underwing
blazed blue as it skims the azure swimming pool.
Past some small blackbirds, and the doctor-bird,
black with a blue face, who works like a bee
the oleander bush; past the cheery
banana-quit, across powdery sand,
raked everyday; and past broad-leaved sea grapes,
squat trees outposted near a ruffling surf:

How are you today? she says, and you say
Thank you, fine, and how are you? and she says
Not as fine as you, and she is right:
you could buy a room in the new hotel,
and she cannot afford the ferry off.
Want my pretty? she says, proffering
her grass baskets, loofahs still in their shells,
and bowls made from the gourds of a calabash tree,
which also serve—she models one—as hats.
Don't want to burn, she says, and even though
your skin has never been so white, so soft,
you tell her Not today, and look at the sea:

past riffling waves, past gulls cresting the tide
like boats, past sun-struck sails, a pencil line

divides dove gray and blue from navy blue,
partitioning the heavens from the earth.
And every day at dusk, released from under
the mangrove's raised umbrella, that cupped hand
overturned and pouring out, bats come
to reattach us—not with the tiny stitches
trawlers make against the far horizon,
but like a loom's ratcheting shuttle, weaving
first a net, then a veil, and then a shroud.

Dooryard Flower

Horace: Ode I.xxxiv

Parcus deorum cultor . . .

Lazy in praising or praying to any god
and madly rational, a clever captain
cruising the open seas of human thought,

now I must bring my vessel full about,
tack into port and sail back out again
on the route from which I strayed. For the God of gods,

who slices through the storm with flashes of fire,
this time in a clear sky came thundering
with his storied horses and his chariot,

whereby the dumb dull earth and its fluttering streams—
and the River Styx, and the dreaded mouth of the cave
at the end of the world—were shaken. So the god

does have sufficient power after all
to turn the tables on both high and low,
the mighty humbled and the meek raised up—

with a swift hiss of her wings, Fortune swoops down,
pleased to place the crown on this one's head,
as she was pleased to snatch it away from that one.

Plaza del Sol

This is a veterans' ward, here by the pool
in Florida, where every chaise is taken, every frame
stretched out to full extension, the bodies just removed
from cold storage, exposing to light and air
the wound, the scar, the birthmark's crushed grape,
contiguous chins undistinguished by pearls,
pitted shoulders plumped or scapular, flesh
pleated under an upper arm, a vast loaf rising
out of the bathing bra, or chest collapsed
and belly preeminent, spine a trough
or a knotted vine climbing the broad cliff-wall.
Down from this pelvic arch five children came;
that suspicious mole, his mother kissed;
but who will finger such calves, their rosaries?
Here's a brace of ankles like water-balloons;
here's a set of toes shingled with horn.
Here is the man, prone, whose back is a pelt,
and the supine woman whose limbs are tinkertoys,
and the man whose tattooed eagle looks crucified,
and his brother with breasts, and his wife with none—
a woman tanned already, dried fruit arranged on a towel—
and her pale sister, seated, bosom piled in her lap,
oiling the lunar landscape of her thighs.
The hot eye over them all does not turn away
from bodies marooned inside loose colorful rags
or bursting their bandages there at the lip of the cave—
from ropy arms, or the heavy sack at the groin,
or the stone of the head—bodies mapped
and marbled, rutted, harrowed, warmed at last,
while everyone else has gone off into the sea.

Anthropology

The large dog sprawls in the road, remembering
his younger triumph over passing cars.
Here comes one now; it swerves, blares its horn,
and his littermate, a smaller quicker dog
trolling the suspect mole, slinks to the porch.
This fails to shame, or teach, or galvanize,
since he would rather be envied than admired—
he holds the road as lion would his rock,
walrus his floe.
                        I knock on the windowpane;
he looks toward me, then turns his thick neck back
to look at the road. I knock again; he looks
at me, then heaves his body up, strolls
to the house with plausible irony: he's not
accountable, who woos whatever traffic
sidles past; whose sleep is comatose
and not disturbed, like hers, by the tic of the hunt;
whose head happens to reach to the willing hand—
my hand rubbing his crown, her currying tongue
all of it costs him nothing. His one job?
To wag his tail when the Alpha Male comes home.
Meanwhile his busy sister patrols the yard,
chases after thunder out in the field,
bites midair in winter the snow-detritus
shuffling from the eaves—she knows she's a dog,
knows what dogs do:
                        hope to please, and plunge.

A Brief Domestic History

A lonely lonely man has come to our door.
He's looking for our friend, the bright penny
he pocketed years ago, who isn't here.
Widow Douglas when our friend was Huck,
and no one else to spend his worry on,
he settles in to wait. He loves to talk—
relieved to leave his solitude on the porch,
beast on a weak leash—and offers up
polished opinions on politics, neighbors, God,
the meal in the firkin; he's Emersonian,
but fond: with my teenaged son, my Bartleby
(whom he thinks is his Thoreau—i.e.,
smart, judgmental, passionate and spoiled),
He talks sports, its algebra. At last,

announced by a shredded muffler, Bright Penny
arrives, at twenty-five all optimistic
energy, lifting the lid off every pot.
Whitmanic, fresh from the world, full of the world,
he tows along a boy he plucked from the ditch
if only to remind him of himself;
they've come for my son, they lob the usual insults
at him, cuff him—the universal greeting—
and then, displacing Lonesome's *gravitas*,
the future commandeers the lit kitchen—
noisy, hungry, hairy, mammalian, gendered
but not entirely sexual, although
there is that carbonation in the air.

Which makes it seem it's the older wounded man
who's Whitman, trying to redirect his need.
Which means the one whose company he seeks,
grown thoughtless from self-reliance, is Emerson,
this time the younger, not afraid of Walt
though distant, proud, as someone's son might be.
So here's Walt/Waldo, abject at forty-eight,
and Waldo/Walt, magnetic at twenty-five,
something passing between them like a wire.
Or maybe an absence, a missing tether, the wire
loose on the ground. Which makes them, all of them, boys,

these two, and of course the even younger two,
my husband, also, just coming in from his lab,
redolent of the power the others covet
thus dismiss—all of them jousting and chafing,
each with his facts, each with his partial story,
none now willing to be seen as ever
odd or sad or lonely, foolish or frightened,
who're gathered at America's long oak table,
ready to fix whatever might be broken,
because I make great soup, great apple pie.

Long Marriage

Forward his numb foot, back
her foot, his chin on her head,
her head on his collarbone,

during those marathons
between wars, our vivid
Dark Times, each dancer holds

the other up so he,
as the vertical heap barely
moves yet moves, or she,

eyes half-lidded, unmoored,
can rest. Why these, surviving
a decimated field?

More than a lucky fit—
not planks planed from the same
oak trunk but mortise and tenon—

it is the yoke that makes
the pair, that binds them to
their blind resolve, two kids

who thought the world was burning
itself out, and bet
on a matched disregard

for the safe and the sad—*Look,*
one hisses toward the flared
familiar ear, *we've come*

this far, this far, this far.

Autumn in the Yard We Planted

Whoever said that I should count on mind?
Think it through, think it up—now that I know so much,
what's left to think is the unthinkable.

And the will has grown too tired to stamp its foot.
It sings a vapid song, it dithers and mopes,
it takes its basket to the marketplace,
like a schoolgirl in her best dress, and watches
others ask outright for what they want—
how do they know what they want?—and haul it away,
the sweet, the dull, the useless and the dear.

A maudlin, whimpering song: in which I lament
my own children, scything their separate paths
into the field, one with steady strokes, one
in a rage. We taught them that. And,
not to look back: at the apple tree, first
to shatter its petals onto the clipped grass,
or the slovenly heads of the russet peonies,

or even that late-to-arrive pastel, all stalk
with a few staggered blossoms, meadow rue—
though surely they could see it from where they are.

Last Letter

A proper interval, and then
you must love twice as hard, and fast.

I dreamed it years ago, more
a feeling than a plotline: I was

invisible and watched it all:
everything the same, the house

our house, children, the shape of the days.
It was summer in the dream, late

dinner on the screened porch, so what
if another woman made the soup,

the salad. I also watched by the bed—
you stroked her with your broad left hand—

and watching, thought: she ought to be glad
I'd broken you in. And felt a rueful

tenderness. And thought, or felt,
she looks like me—and so the dream

pleased me with its flattery.
But now I think, better what

you didn't have, and recommend
pliant and serene, perhaps

a little blithe. That bright morning
after the dream, the dream rushed back

only when I had stood, unthinking,
in the hot shower, and at its touch,

wept, like blown glass shattering,
before the narrative, remembered,

told me why. My weeping's done.
You will have the harder task,

it's true, but don't you see? Your need
will be your tribute, my legacy.

Horace: Ode I.xxxvii

Nunc est bibendum . . .

Now it's time to drink, now loosen your shoes
and dance, now bring around elaborate couches
and set the gods a feast, my friends! Before,

the time wasn't right to pour the vintage wines,
not while that queen and her vile brood of advisors,
dizzy with desire and drunk on luck,
were busy in deluded plots against us.

What sobered her up was seeing her fleet on fire—
hardly a ship survived—nightmare she woke to
sending her fleeing, flying, from our shores,

Caesar at the oars in close pursuit—
the way the hawk harasses the helpless dove,
or the hunter the hare in the snow-packed open field—
intent on dragging the monster back in chains.

And yet the death that she resolved was grand:
a woman who did not shrink from the drawn blade,
who did not try to slip away and hide,

she looked straight at the palace now in ruins,
her face composed, and without blinking took
into her arms the scaly venomous snakes
in order to drink each drop of their black wine,

and by that cup this woman of such fierce pride
made the triumph hers: that she would die
not as a slave, and not as someone's prize.

What I Remember of Larry's Dream of Yeats

A roomful of writers, three on the couch a cat
had pissed on, others clustered like animated trees,
Shahid benched at the melodiophobic piano
Reg had played while Deb and Karen sang;
and centered, under the fixture overhead, Larry,
pleated around a straight-backed chair, not drinking
then, not doing dope, his face above the mustache open
for company—although I heard him tell the dream
in North Carolina, after he moved to Virginia,

he'd dreamed it long before in Salt Lake City.
"Things not going very well," he summarized,
hurrying to what would make us laugh: him alone
and broke and barely hanging on, Strand advising
"'Buy silk sheets.'" I've forgotten whether or not
he did, whether or not the stained mattress
had been sheathed in silk, because he so expertly
buried for us that bed in papers, notebooks, volumes
underlined, low mound of the written word

as erudite, disheveled as Larry was,
taking a turn in the light of our attention, T-shirt
even though it was winter, distressed gray hair.
"In the midst of this" (here he lit another smoke),
"I'd been preparing for my class on Yeats," days, nights
on guided tours of the Variorum and *A Vision*;
also in the layers, the *L.A. Times*, manuscripts of poems
(his students' and his own), clean and dirty laundry,
letters, bills, an opened bag of chips.

Both white feet splayed flat on the splintered floor,
forearms on his knees, he leaned forward, maybe
to give this part some shoring-up, since labor
ran counter to his irony, his off-the-cuff,
his disaffected style—but didn't he know we knew
intelligence as restless and large as his
needs feeding from time to time? (What did Dobyns say:
a billion who ought to die before Larry did?) Besides,
he looked so much like a caught thief coming clean,

none of us doubted he had read it all,
everything on Yeats, and fell asleep, and Yeats
stopped by, wearing a white suit. He'd come to retrieve
a last still-undiscovered poem, which he happened to keep
in Utah, in a locked drawer in Larry's room—just then
the kitchen howled and hooted, as if Larry
had also been in *there*, doing Justice, teacher
he loved, as an ice-cream man. Here's when Dr. Orlen
entered the room, stirring a short Scotch-rocks,

and Larry double-stitched: "Yeats in white,
pointing at my notes: 'Why do you bother with *that*?'"
Pause. Larry stared at Tony, next at me, the three of us
sharing the one ashtray, his eyebrows up, accents
acute et grave, like facing, aggressive bears:
"'Passion,' Yeats said, 'is all that matters in poetry.'"
Trawling the line to see if we would bite,
he leaned back in the chair, chair on its hind legs,
his legs straight out, his mouth a puckered seam.

In the dream Yeats turned away, as we ourselves
were starting to turn away now from the dream, to reach
for another fistful of chips or Oreos, another humiliation
from the Poetry Wars, another sensual or shapely thing
to throw at loneliness or grief, like what I'll hear
from Mary Flinn, how, when Richmond's ROBINSON'S REMOVAL
came for the body, days still undiscovered on the floor,
to wrestle it like a sodden log out to the hearse,
they swaddled it first in a scarlet velvet tarp,

then aimed for the stairs, headlong, the tapered end
under the arm of a ravaged small thin old black man
(that's Robinson), his doughy-bosomed lieutenant at the helm,
and Mary, foot of the stairs and looking up, expecting
Larry to break loose any minute, tumble forward—
the kind of punchline we were avid for
that evening in Swannanoa with good friends
(was Heather there? was Lux fanning the fire?) when Larry
pulled himself upright and dropped his voice

as Yeats paused at the door in a white silk suit:
ancient, graveled, this was the voice of the caged sibyl,
shriveled the size of a flea, when he read, from his long poem,
her song, "I want to die"; and saying now, as Yeats, " 'Passion
is also all that matters in *life*.' "

                          So weren't the dream,
and the telling of the dream, more lanky shrewd inclusive
Levis poems, like those in his books, those he left
in the drawer? If he comes to get them, let him come
in his usual disguise: bare feet, black clothes.

Dooryard Flower

Because you're sick I want to bring you flowers,
flowers from the landscape that you love—
because it is your birthday and you're sick
I want to bring outdoors inside,
the natural and wild, picked by my hand,
but nothing is blooming here but daffodils,
archipelagic in the short green
early grass, erupted
bulbs planted decades before we came,
the edge of where a garden once was kept
extended now in a string of islands I straddle
as in a fairy tale, harvesting,
not taking the single blossom from a clump
but thinning where they're thickest, tall-stemmed
from the mother patch, dwarf to the west, most
fully opened, a loosened whorl,
one with a pale spider luffing her thread,
one with a slow beetle chewing the lip, a few
with what's almost a lion's face, a lion's mane,
and because there is a shadow on your lungs, your liver,
and elsewhere, hidden,
some of those with delicate green
streaks in the clown's ruff (corolla—
actually made from adapted leaves), and more
right this moment starting to unfold, I've gathered
my two fists full, I carry them like a bride,
I am bringing you the only glorious thing
in the yards and fields between my house and yours,
none of the tulips budded yet, the lilac

a sheaf of sticks, the apple trees
withheld, the birch unleaved—
it could still be winter here, were it not
for green dotted with gold, but you won't wait
for dogtooth violets, trillium under the pines,
and who could bear azaleas, dogwood, early profuse rose
of somewhere else when you're assaulted here, early May,
not any calm narcissus, orange *corona*
on scalloped white, not even its slender stalk
in a fountain of leaves, no stiff cornets of the honest
jonquils, gendered parts upthrust in brass and cream:
just this common flash in anyone's yard,
scrambled cluster of petals
crayon-yellow, as in a child's drawing of the sun,
I'm bringing you a sun, a children's choir, host
of transient voices, first bright
splash in the gray exhausted world, a feast
of the dooryard flower we call butter-and-egg.

MESSENGER: NEW POEMS

(2006)

Francis

The Feeder

Bright blossom on the shrub's green lapel—
within hours after we hang the feeder
beside the wild viburnum, a goldfinch lights there.

And then, next day, a rose-breasted grosbeak
posing for us, making us proud as though
we'd painted ourselves the bloody bib
on its puffed white chest: our first failing.
                                        Our second:
disappointment with the chickadees—
common and local—despite the sleek black cap,
clean white cheeks, acrobatic body.

But weren't the early gifts a promise?
We've hung fat meat from a nearby branch, wanting
large, crested, rare, rapturous,
redbird fixed on the bush like a ripe fruit.

2

Whenever the grosbeak comes, he comes
with his harem, lumps plain as sparrows,

and doesn't merely eat but preens,
never to be mistaken for some other.

The goldfinch likes to travel in flocks—
several indelible males, jostling,

careening up to the feeder, then away,
each a child on a stick, galloping;

and females, less spectacular,
shades of green and brown mixed into the yellow,

better to subside into the foliage.

3

It struts on the grass, like a crow but smaller,
or, the grackle, whose green head shines,
or the starling, aiming its golden eye,

or the red-winged with its gaudy flags,
but this bird, this bird crosses the grass
white stripe tucked, the orange locked up.

Blackbird, blackbird, fly away.
Take sorrow with you when you go.
Raven, starling, grackle, crow.

Tricolored Blackbird, my favorite, my signature:
nobody knows for sure what it is
till it flies away.

4

O poor little bird, little dull peewee
with your condescending name—

is it enough merely to sing
with such a transparent song?

5

Some: thistle; some: sunflower, cracked, already shelled.
But it's grease that wooed these out of the woods,
a pair, Hairy not Downy, we know this
from their size and not their call.

Why are they squeaking? Bigger
than the rest, not bullied by jays, seizing the stash,
swinging on it, drilling into it, one at a time
as the other clings to the trunk of the nearest pine
and waits its turn,
                              even the one with the red
slash on his head.

6

Today: one wild turkey, more a meal than a bird,

refusing to stay with the others out in the field
bobbing for apples—
                              bobbing *up*, from a crouch
on the crusted snowpack, olympic leaps.
                                        They also fly,
improbable and brutally efficient, low to the ground;

and the tree they roost in
trembles.

7

Late March: glazed over, here,
don't go near Virginia—

that stab of forsythia, cherry weeping,
redbud smeared on the hill,

and perched in my sister's dogwood,
seven elegant cardinals, each

wearing a crown like something
it had earned, and trumpeting.

8

Suddenly there suddenly gone.

                                  Do they count

if they come not to the back yard but the front,

not to the feeder but the crabapple tree,

its ornaments dulled

by winter?

                  Multiple, tufted,

pulled forward by the blunt beak

like dancers propelled by the head:

                                  cedar waxwings:

I almost missed them, looking the other way.

9

Nothing at the feeder. Nothing at the bush.
It takes awhile before I see the shadow.

10

So: she's found me here:
chief bird of my childhood,
gray, pillow-breasted,
only needed asking—
no, only the crumbs
of others' invitations.
She waddles beneath the feeder,
retrieving what she can
from the hulls, the debris dropped
to the grass by the glamorous birds,
thrusting her undersized head
forward and back, forward
and back again. And her call,
alto, cello, *tremolo,*
makes the life I've made
melt away.

Deathbed

He woke from fitful sleep, his father said,
calling for his mother—why wasn't she there,
why would she leave him in darkness and in pain?

"And I had to tell him, as if for the first time—
it was for him again the first time—
his mother had long been dead. For me, that loss

had become a shard worn smooth inside my pocket.
For him, it was sharp, new, not possible.
He wailed like a baby, my poor bewildered child,

and could not be consoled, like a child."

The Hive

To do something with it: to make something of it:
language races alongside, any given minute,

anything that happens—flies ahead of it
or lags behind, looking for meaning, beyond us yet,

on which we feed. So when the child provides the perfect
utterance, at once profound and innocent, resident

mystic, parent thinks, *got to write that down.* Next step:
dinner party, rude guest, appalled wife of guest,

the spilled red wine, congealed meat, the spoils left
to be distilled by the host *on whom nothing is lost.*

And what if the wife or even the self-afflicted guest
is you? Or, if your friend/wife/mother has been beset:

you drive to Intensive Care and take along a book:
worse, you take your pencils—two, in case one breaks—

and little bits of paper handy in your pocket,
are you not a monster? But is the human mind not

monstrous in its secret appetites, its habits?
In the Common Room, room soured by hope, late at night,

intending kind distraction, you hear your own mouth asking
the father of Frank, who is dying, "what do you do for a *living,*"

the unforgivable word a marker for the thought:
however will he/would I survive? Monstrous to set

that thought aside. But on your barely legible scraps:
the phrases, the very words, preserved like bees trapped

in amber, in anger, in grief, in all that overwhelmed.
Again, again, again, frail wings beat as they hover

over the untranslated world, to find what we need
(*thicket blooming south of here*) and bring what they find

back to the humming, hungry, constricted hive.

Harvesting the Cows

Stringy, skittery, thistle-burred, rib-etched,
   they're like a pack of wolves lacking a sheep
      but also lacking the speed, the teeth, the wits—

they're heifers culled from the herd, not worth the cost
   of feeding and breeding and milking, let loose on a hill
      one-third rock, one-third blackberry bramble.

And now, the scrub stung black by hard frost,
   here come the young farmer and his father,
      one earnest, one wizened, wind-whipped, sun-whipped,

who make at the gate, from strewn boards and boughs,
   a pen, and park at its near end the compact
      silver trailer, designed for two horses—

it waits at the mouth of the rutted tractor-trail
   descending through trees, an artificial gulley.
      Up goes Junior, hooting, driving them down.

So much bigger than wolves, these sixteen cows:
   head to flank or flank to scrawny flank,
      they can't turn around; but what they know is *no*:

some splash over the walls of the small corral,
   one, wall-eyed, giddy, smashes away
      the warped plank that's propped on the far side,

crashing across alders and wet windfall
in a plausible though explosive dance, which prompts
another to aim herself at the same hole,

too late: the plank's back up, she's turned to the clump
and soon swimming among them, their white necks
extended like the necks of hissing geese,

but so much bigger than geese. When the younger man
wraps one neck in his arms, the cow rears up
and he goes down, plaid wool in shit-slicked mud;

so then the elder takes her by the nose—
I mean, he puts two fingers and a thumb
inside the nostrils, pulls her into the trailer.

The rest shy and bunch away from the gate;
a tail lifts for a stream of piss; one beast
mounts another—panic that looks erotic—

and the herdsmen try guile, a pail of grain
kept low, which keeps the head of the lead cow low
as though resigned, ready for the gallows.

The silver loaf opens, swallows them in,
two by two by two, and takes them away.
Hams need to be smoked, turkeys to be dressed out

here in Arcadia, where a fine cold spit
    needles the air, and the birch and beech let go
        at last their last tattered golden rags.

Rubato

For the action: hammers of walnut—*nussbaum,* "nut tree";
the pinblock, hard-grained beech;

the keyframe, oak; the keybed, pine;
the knuckles, rosewood. In the belly, to ripen the tone,

maple, mahogany, and ironwood,
also called "hornbeam." The soundboard

spruce, best ratio of strength to weight, once split
not sawed, strip after narrow strip,

one-ply like the back of a cello, pressed together,
over which the struck strings quiver.

Two years after her only brother died,
Papa, prosperous, took her to Berlin
to the factory, pianos fresh from the forest.
Inside: sound of the burr and chisel.

In her sailor dress and straight blunt-cut black hair,
she tried the one too bright, the one too dark,
choosing *this* one, head bent over the keyboard,
lost inside her *Kinderszenen*

as the clerks, gathered to listen, drew up the papers,
and Papa, patting his weskit, smiling again,
shipped it home by train to Wagenfeld.
Lodged inside: first love, first power.

Then shipped it back to Berlin in '29:
she'd stamped her teenaged foot for the *avant garde,*
to be let loose in Berlin *unter den linden.*
Locked inside: her mother's weeping.

Then shipped it ahead of her to America,
with linens, crystal, silver, fine bone china,
what I married into, crates of Rhein wine.
Inside: "Rhapsody in Blue"—

3

not what my parents might have played
if my father had ever learned how to play
and if my mother had ever played

anything other than her one song,
"The Moon Shines Tonight on Pretty Red Wing,"
which may have been the very song

she played the evening they first met,
playing it over the years on the prized upright
bought "on time," egg-money spent

on their three children, what they chose
when it still seemed the future could be chosen,
the world waiting for what they'd choose.

4

Deep in Robert Schumann's Piano Concerto,
at the cadenza's end, the violins
at rest, bows lowered into their laps, and the Maestro
cradling his baton, the two French horns
shaking their spit out onto the floor, the oboe
keeping his reed moist in his mouth—when the grand
returns, after the solo *appassionato*,
triplets now set against the bold left hand,

when they pull themselves again to full attention,
ready to reinstate the common measure,
they first must listen and wait, wait and listen,
all forward movement stalled, while the piano
lists wheresoever she will: tempo rubato:
time taken from one note, given to another.

5

More like the Amazon flute than the silver flute,
a layered sound and not a brilliant sound,

the Bechstein's rim being "radiant" not "reflective,"
not continuous but joined, the joint
where the box housing the action meets the curve.

Before it was ours we made for it a second
radiant chamber, one wall spruce, one pine,
scraping past the pastel cabbage roses,

the sheep-on-a-hill, the girl behind her hat
as in my parents' bedroom, the painted plaster.
Then sanded down the grain and oiled it back,

once a day for a week, once a week
for a month, each month for a year, year after year.

Also for the action: to settle the hammers
and speed each note's decay: tiny leather
tethers, and nestled nearby, to absorb and cushion,
glued inside: felts made of wool,

as from the mill in Wagenfeld, known
for durable blankets. Or felts that were made of hair,
pallets of hair—think of what might sleep
inside Grandmother's Chesterfield,

and think of the shorn heads turned into ash,
Papa and Mama smuggled out through Spain,
the mill seized, *das Juden* scrawled on the wall;
inside: the songs of Mendelssohn.

And her first language bitter on her tongue,
her marriage growing decadent, remote,
her hands growing slowly stiff and gnarled;
inside: Brahms' last Capriccio;

and the wine waiting under the cellar stairs,
and three sons born and all of them insufficient,
and Wagenfeld long gone with its cupolas;
inside: Schumann's "Träumerei";

and Papa gone, and Mama mute from a stroke,
and the corks rotted, the wine now vinegar,

the Bechstein's action sludge, its soundboard cracked;
inside: Beethoven's "Pathétique."

7

How many times the same imperative:
coming with younger brothers home from school,
finding the note propped on the shut piano
that must have seemed when she wrote it rational,
and then the siren, the deep chagrin, life
taken up again—
                            no wonder you hate "drama,"
any passionate speech "hysterical"
or worse: deliberate, someone's "agenda."

So the past is not a scar but a wound:
I've seen it breaking open.

8

Every day since 1931,
the year your parents met under the lindens,

the year my parents met in someone's kitchen,
our neighbor born next door has written down

the weather in our little town, the weddings,
the births and deaths—it is, whatever the season,

the daily song she sings, and we are in it, our daughter, our son,
his daughter. Today, that child turns one

so I play Grieg, her countryman,
then play Schumann's "Kinderszenen,"

and then: ragtime, American stride left hand
a steady measurement, the free right hand

a stitch ahead of the beat, then a stitch behind,
the stammered math of feeling

while the chords, in their circle of fifths, shift down,
and you come down the stairs in your pajamas, listening—

it's a new song when someone listens—
as when my father brought me Sunday's hymn,

and we sat together at the cheap upright, on the narrow bench,
side by side like two birds on a branch

facing into the wind, and I played for him
note by hammered note the baritone.

Redbud

Everywhere, like grass: toadflax, yellow coils
      a girl's pincurls. Overhead,
the purely ornamental fruits, whites and pinks

thick on the bough. And straight ahead, along the path,
      spice viburnum, exotic shrub
named for the smell its clustered flowers held—nutmeg—

that made St. Louis tropical. We walked a lush,
      vast, groomed preserve—*preserve* in the sense
meant by self-indulgent kings, and in the sense

meant by science: every bloom and bine and bole,
      each independent green was labeled,
that was what we loved. And at the center, bronzed:

Linnaeus, master of design, whose art it was
      to shepherd any living thing
into its proper pasture. There, foamflower. There,

lungwort, vernacular "Spilled Milk," leaf splashed with white,
      a graceful *pulmonaria*
in the language of greatest clarity which classifies

lilies and roses, rows of lilac. And here, at our feet,
      shade-drunk dark herb: wormwood, our word
for bitterness: an *Artemisia*, The Hunter,

goddess made incarnate on the ground, in whose name
        the avid mortal watching her
was torn apart. Where was *his* name? Where was his flower?

A cloud paused in the spring sky, and there came to us then,
        on the path, another blossoming.
Radiant in mauve, head to toe, back braced

as though to balance the weight of full breasts, one hand,
        gloved, lifted unthinking to pet
the back of the hair, the hair itself a lacquered helmet.

And what should we make of her height, her heft, the size of the feet,
        the gruff swagger in the gait:
we stared outright—it seemed all right to stare, like

Linnaeus, who'd ranked the stones, and sorted the plants by how
        they propagate and colonized
whatever crawls and swims and flies and bears live young?

Light by which I've lived, the wish to name, to know,
        the work of it, the cost of it—
if only I could be, or want to be, more like

that boy: ignorant, stunned, human.
                        "Acteon," you said,
        by his own hounds torn asunder. And so
the brief shadow flickered and dissolved: the world

was ours again, the world like *this*, made less confused.
    And we strolled like kings back down the path,
past a redbud tree in plush white bloom.

The Tattered Dress

The day the royal court came through our village—
many drums and flutes, grandfather monkeys
with faces like fists and jewels the size of fists,
each elephant its own tree of blossoms,
a tiger on a leash, a pair of peacocks—

the old emperor did not choose me:
he chose my delicate sister. Our poor family
shrieked and clapped and pulled their hair, thinking,
plenty rice each year. And what does *she* think,
in the emperor's lap, inside the palace walls?

I did not put away the beautiful clothes
but wear them out among the buffalo,
wear them out in the field, in the standing water,
the filthy water that breeds our meat and drink,
my bent back a flash of scarlet and gold

that scatters the ducks and aggravates the swine.
Why not? Do I have some other calling?
The dull human oxen point at me:
one-almost-chosen: what
the lesser gods thought I could withstand.

Their judgment too I can withstand.

Prayer

Artemis—virginal goddess of the hunt, thus
    goddess of childbirth, protector of children, to whom
        agonized women can cry out—

was not a name I thought of, a place to send
    those sharp gasps, when you descended sideways,
        still swimming against the narrow walls of me;

or later, after, the low moans, the mews,
    as I throbbed like something flung from a great height
        and could not be appeased; or in between,

a keening, you by then presenting, the cord—
    the lifeline, tether, leash—lashed like a noose
        round and round your neck by so much swimming.

I think what I said, if saying is what I did,
    was *Sweet Jesus,* another virgin who knew
        the body is first and last an animal,

it eats, shits, fucks, expels the fetus—or doesn't.
    Midnight, lamplight in the barn, the farmer,
        arm deep in the cow, turning, turning the calf;

and my father, a farmer, phoning up to ask
    what had gone wrong, he could not keep his worry
        out of his voice. Perhaps I should have prayed

to him, or to some other powerful god
      assigned to *me,* when you were stalled
         inside the birth canal; and also:

when they ripped you out and cut us free.

Adagio

We never said aloud: into the earth or fire.
And if earth, then where. And if fire, then where

to cast the ashes.

Each thought the other would choose: choosing for two, not one—
the body lying flat, the body left upright.

And if a stone.

Messenger

1

First I smelled it, hovering near the bed:
distinctly saline, as in a ship's wake;

a bit of dust and mold, like moth-found fur;
also something grassy, crushed herb, sharper.

After that, when they turned the ward lights out,
the spaceship glowing at the nurses' hub,

his pod stilled and darkened, only the small
digitals updating on the screen,

then I could see—one "sees" in deep gloaming,
though ground-fog makes an airless, formless room—

how fully it loomed behind and larger than
the steel stalk, the sweet translucent fruit.

One doesn't notice wings when they're at rest.
One doesn't notice the scythe of the beak at rest:

opaque, like horn, or bone, knobbed at the base
but tapering, proportionate to the head.

In Quattrocento paintings, Mary's face
is mirrored by the messenger's radiant face:

that's meant to comfort—*see, they're just like us.*
No, they're not like us. This had no face,

and its posture was a suspect courtesy,
stolen from a courtier who nods

to the aging king, head bowed, and holds aside,
lowered, but unsheathed, the sword.

2

Except in wired emergencies, the signals
   sounding for a pressure drop but not
      a fever spike, a bad white count, blood
         transfused too fast, a tube dislodged, sudden
            struggle to breathe, the opiates late again,
               always late—it was my task to harry
                  the Duty-Nurse, Charge-Nurse, Intern, Attending,
                  to put in the rut of their path implacable me—

the workers came and went without alarm
   and thus I could not trust them—
                         they must think it
   part of the common furniture that clutters
cardio-thoracic post-surgical wards,

but I think not: I think your father's code
   was branded somewhere on its bony leg,
      631688, the same sign
         stamped on the band clamped to the swollen wrist,
        markers for an arduous migration.
          I think it was used to hunger. I think it was waiting
            for me to leave the room.

3

01-21-05.   0400.
Before the workers came for vital signs,
halfway through the IV bag's collapse,

the cuff tightening on his good right arm,
a little purr, a read-out click on the wall,
then a hush, no anguish from his or other pods,

I think it moved. At least I can say I heard
a faint new noise:
                        as if a great blue heron,
not nesting but next to the nest, an eye on the nest,
still as a stalk beside the water's edge,
resting on one leg, had stirred.

4

That all this happened far away from you;
that the verb "think" is stupid and unworthy;
that when all this began, the world went away;
that what we thought the world was, was a dream;
that you, the hub of that world, belong to the dream;
that you, remembered, now must be imagined;
that imagining is how we think we choose;
that the verb "choose" is stupid and unworthy;
that need, unspeakable need, is what imagines
while joy or grief, rage or terror dreams;
that there is no world except the worlds we dream;
that while I imagine you you're dreaming us;
that in the dream you dream your father rises.

5

Birds migrate in flocks, there was no flock.

When we moved out, into the strange city,
    and I became the lone worker-bee,
        my queen—your father—fixed in the high bed,

above his heart the violent slash, cross-hatched,
    above his heart tattoos for the next aggression,
        above his heart a major vein now missing,

the oxygen-machine a lullaby,
    shush-shush, the multiple colorful pills piled
        in labeled boxes, our calendar and clock—

it didn't go back, legs dangling down like commas,
    without the soul it might have carried like lice
        below a wing, kept warm beneath its feathers:

it followed us there, and stood in the rented yard
    behind the live oaks and the oleander—
        I saw it once, I'd learned where I should look.

And when, that season ended, we came home,
    it came too. From the kitchen window, west,
        down the sledding hill to the berry-bramble,

you'd see where: in early dark, camouflaged
 among the gaunt gray alders along the brook,
  still as a stalk beside the water's edge—

of course it's there. It winters over.

HEADWATERS

(2013)

Headwaters

I made a large mistake I left my house I went into the world it was not
the most perilous hostile part but I couldn't tell among the people there

who needed what no tracks in the snow no boot pointed toward me or away
no snow as in my dooryard only the many currents of self-doubt I clung

to my own life raft I had room on it for only me you're not surprised
it grew smaller and smaller or maybe I grew larger and heavier

but don't you think I'm doing better in this regard I try to do better

Privet Hedge

first frail green in the northeast the forest around us no longer
a postcard of Christmas snow clotting the spruce or worse
fall's technicolor beeches sumac sugar maple death
even the death of vegetation should never be
so beautiful it is unseemly I prefer the cusps
they focus the mind
                              which otherwise stays
distracted knowing things when my friend said
knowledge does nothing for him I felt at once superior
and chastised I'd just deduced the five new birds in my yard
woodpecker size and stripes and red blaze but feeding on the ground
five yellow-shafted flickers can the soul be known by its song who hears it
what keeps it aloft what keeps it whole what helps it survive habitual
pride greed wrath sloth lust a list compiled by a parent always
needing something to forgive you for I meant

to ask the nuns to straighten this out for me
while I was among them in Minnesota their earlier spring
but I couldn't guess which ones they are they dress
like everyone else no veils no starched white
no kneeling boards I was left on my own
to study the graveyard behind the privet hedge

their markers all alike as on a battlefield immense and calm
beneath an open midwestern sky nothing between
the pilgrim and the scoured horizon

Stones

birds not so much the ducks and geese okay not horses cows pigs
she'd lived in the city all her life some cats and dogs okay as part

of someone else's narrative the posted photographs are someone's
pets the figurines less figurative than graceful to behold the same

with carved giraffes and camels no reptiles no amphibians nothing
from the sea although she loved the sea her passion was for stones

I don't know why the parquet floor never buckled and caved collapsed
into the rooms below her rooms all the horizontal surfaces were covered

with stones the bureau the cupboards the closets were full of the precious
stones she wore at her throat her ears her fingers her wrists the inlaid

tables held ceramic bowls of polished stones the antique desk a basket
of stones a bushel of stones on the floor on the windowsills more stones

each one unique each one a narrative the étagère held up to the light stones
hewn from the source and hauled up here still jagged refracting light in every

shade of amethyst her birthstone like my mother's crystals shimmering
as if alive rescued from the field the cliff the shore the riverbed I found

a single cufflink by her bed a tiny diamond set in silver did her father sift out
at his flour mill the dangerous stones I stretched out beside her in her bad time

thinking to help her sleep I held her hand her fingers wore a few
of her favorite rings the two of us lay entirely still atop the quilt

a stiff sarcophagus she didn't sleep her mind was an etched plate
from which she drew off print after print the framed prints on the walls

were all interiors our talk had always been a stone kicked down a hill
no purpose no destination her father her mother my mother my dogs

she never said she was leaving me in charge she wasn't my mother why
put me in charge I put the jewels on other throats and wrists I threw away

the bushels of cosmetics and perfume her chosen armaments
against the world who loved the world I sold the breakfront

cabinet full of cut glass bowls and blown glass figurines but who
will save the living stones she loved I have so many already

in my yard half-in half-out of the earth immovable
she'd seen my yard she'd seen those heavy stones

Oak

not to board the bus but wait for the last bell
like those who live in town shuffling ahead of her the clumps
drift apart drift back shifting boys in a cluster now a boy and a girl
a dance a recess game as each is subtracted one by one into the houses
she passes the windows half-lidded by half-drawn shades
or framed by curtains and sash she likes

                                 walking alone
along the verge of the lawns no fence no field the leaves
drifting out from under the oaks while in the woods
they would only settle and rot she likes the way a passing car
releases them across the grid of the sidewalk a solid math
for a solitary girl the small steps into the larger
world of strangers wholly indifferent houses cars rust-colored dog
she passes the hardware grocery pharmacy beauty salon every Thursday
you've noticed such a child content to be invisible
scuffing the leaves

                     toward the bungalow the hushed backroom
where someone is propped in the high bed her webbed face
her halo of hair past humankind and all its suffering
past seeing now past death too old for death
and waiting for this girl

                    who thumbs the latch
who lifts the lid of the black box lifts from red felt those silver pieces
fits them together the trick is to breathe across and not directly
into the small round hole as her arched fingers hover
over the other open holes each finger knows its task she's fixed
to one purpose *Joyful Joyful We Adore Thee*

dark out in the street the wind ruffling oak leaves the dark
window lit by the silver flute the white ghost hair the brighter
lights is it her mother come to drive her home

My Mother

my mother my mother my mother she
could do anything so she did everything the world
was an unplowed field a dress to be hemmed a scraped knee it needed
a casserole it needed another alto in the choir her motto was apply yourself
the secret of life was spreading your gifts why hide your light
under a bushel you might

forget it there in the dark times the lonely times
the sun gone down on her resolve she slept a little first
so she'd be fresh she put on a little lipstick drawing on her smile
she pulled that hair up off her face she pulled her stockings on she stepped
into her pumps she took up her matching purse already
packed with everything they all would learn
they would be nice they would

apologize they would be grateful whenever
they had forgotten what to pack she never did
she had a spare she kissed your cheek she wiped the mark
away with her own spit she marched you out again unless you were
that awful sort of stubborn broody child who more and more
I was who once had been so sweet so mild staying put
where she put me what happened

must have been the bushel I was hiding in
the sun gone down on her resolve she slept a little first
so she'd be fresh she pulled her stockings on she'd packed
the words for my every lack she had a little lipstick on her teeth the mark
on my cheek would not rub off she gave the fluids from her mouth
to it she gave the tissues in her ample purse to it I never did

apologize I let my sister succor those in need and suffer
the little children my mother

knew we are self-canceling she gave herself
a lifetime C an average grade from then on out she kept
the lights on day and night a garden needs the light the sun
could not be counted on she slept a little day and night she didn't need
her stockings or her purse she watered she weeded she fertilized she stood
in front the tallest stalk keeping the deer the birds all
the world's idle shameless thieves away

Owl

the sign for making the most of what you have
on the human hand is a thumb at full right angle to the palm
for the owl it's two talons forward two back a flexible foot
that crushes the prey and lifts it to the beak to the eyes
which are legally blind this is why the owl

hunts in the dark in the dusk when nothing is clearly seen
and why the owl's eyes are fixed facing ahead to better focus
so its whole face swivels in each direction like the turret on a tank
the round plates of feathers surrounding the eyes collect the least sound
when it turns the owl is computing by geometry the exact

location of the mouse or snake or songbird
that moves imperceptibly in its nest toward which the owl
sets out from the hole in the tree the burrow the eave of the barn
and crosses the field in utter silence wing-feathers overlapped
to make no sound poor mouse poor rabbit
                                        last night
from the porch obbligato to the brook and the snuffling deer
intent on the gnarled worm-bitten apples we leave on the tree
I heard what must have been a Barred Owl or a Barn Owl
or a Lesser Horned Owl close by not deep in the woods
what I heard was less a call than a cry

a fragment repeating repeating a kind of shudder
which may be why the country people I come from
thought an owl was prescient ill-omen meant to unspool
the threads they'd gathered and wound I was a grown woman
when my father took the key from under the eave

and unlocked the door to the darkened house he had grown up in
and stepped across the threshold and said as he entered the empty room
hello Miss Sally as though his stepmother dead for weeks
were still in her usual chair
                              in the Medicine Wheel
the emblem for wisdom is the same for gratitude at dusk at dark
the farsighted owl strikes in utter silence when we hear it
from the tree or the barn what it announces
is already finished

Milkmaid

white froth overnight on bare ground brown leaves
no yellow bus on the snow-slicked road so I could help my father
deliver the mail his other job begin at six finish at two then farm

my part was laboring through the drifts
toward the red flag the widow's flag meant
dried-apple pies fried pockets of fruit to sweeten

his usual bitter thermos his usual two sandwiches
one butter sliced in a slab the peasant's cheese one meat
maybe headcheese the leftover parts of pig snowdays

I wore his fishing boots rolled at my waist
I waded to the metal box put something in took something out
I still believe getting the mail is the best part of the day my belovèd

disagrees he says he has enough bad news but what about finding
among the trash a piece of smooth beach glass today a postcard
a milkmaid's royal blue emphatic apron

not dulled by many washings not stained by milk or mud the blue
Vermeer's ennoblement he lets her pour a pure white stream
from the lip of the pitcher into the earthbrown bowl

what's rich has been set aside for butter or cheese
what's left enough to soften the week's stale bread a peasant's
Sunday supper Milk Soup my father's favorite

Yearling

Thanksgiving Day was the day they slaughtered the hog the carcass
hoisted by its heels from the oak the planks across sawhorses holding
the hams the buckets catching the blood the shanks the organ meats
the chunks of white fat for biscuits the feet sunk in brine while the yard-dogs
whined for the leathery ear and my grandmother napped
with the baby always a baby needing a nap

                                                my neighbor
at ninety-six claims she's never had a nap she has no use for dogs
she used to spend Thanksgiving in the woods getting her deer
and strung it up outside the shed where now droops
head down rack down her son's deer her knives
stay sharp one year her son brought by

not venison a yearling bear glossy and black dressed out
there wasn't much underneath its thick coat
a scrawny frame the paws so much like hands she said
when she looked through the window it startled her
hanging there the size of a child

Cow

end of the day daylight subsiding into the trees lights coming on
in the milking barns as somewhere out in the yard some ants
are tucking in their aphids for the night behind
hydrangea leaves or in their stanchions underground
they have been bred for it the smaller brain

serving the larger brain the cows eat so we will eat we guarantee
digestion is the only work they do heads down tails up
they won't have sex they get some grain some salt
no catamounts no wolves we fertilize the fields
we put up bales of hay we give them names

but again this week one breached the fence the neighbors
stopped to shoo it back a girl held out a handful of grass
calling the cow as you would a dog no dice so what
if she recoiled to see me burst from the house with an ax
I held it by the blade I tapped with the handle where the steaks come from

like the one I serve my friend a water sign who likes to lurk
in the plural solitude of Zen retreat to calm his mind but when it's done
what he needs I think is something truly free of mind a slab of earth
by way of cow by way of fire the surface charred the juices
running pink and red on the white plate

Fox

rangy loping swiveling left then right I'm thinking
nonchalant but the doves flutter up to the roof of the barn the crickets
leap from the grass like fleas a fox is in my yard-o my yard-o
plenty of songs in my head

to sing to my child's child if she were here
she wakes in her wooden crib and sings to herself
odd happy child so like another child content in her pen
with a pot a metal straw a lid a hole in the lid a glass hat
for the hole a metal basket with smaller holes
one hole the size of the straw for hours

I made the pieces fit then took them apart
then made them fit when I got tired I lay me down my little head
against the flannel chicks and ducks then slept then woke then took
the puzzle up my mother had another child sick unto death
she needed me to fall in love with solitude I fell in love
it is my toy my happiness the child of my friends
is never ever left alone asleep awake
pushing her wooden blocks around the rug they cannot bear
her least distress their eyes stay on their sparrow poor happy child

last year I startled a fox crossing the road the tail
more rust than red the head cranked forward facing me
it stopped stock-still as if deciding whether to hurry forward
or turn back it had a yellow apple in its mouth
and the little ones chew on the bones-o

Noble Dog

behind our house down to the brook and the woods
beyond the groomed grass and flower beds what we see
are brook and woods and sometimes mild creatures of the field
we thought when we bathed in the claw-footed tub we could pretend
we stayed inside the natural world no shutters no shades at night

beside the mirror over the sink the windows darkened into mirrors
where my daughter at thirteen admired her tan her new body until she felt
or thought she felt something move outside in the yard and asked quietly
up the backstairs for us to come down here for just a minute please
come down here now we couldn't tell how much was fear

how much was shame we thought she needed us to be calm
we tried to be calm like the trooper we called who said without alarm
to the handsome noble dog where is he buddy where is he buddy
at which as if in a game of fetch the dog went straight around the house
to the one smell that didn't fit to the one smell that crossed the clipped grass

into the ditch beside the dirt road where the dog went too the dog
tracking the smell the trooper tracking the dog the dog
not barking or baying until the scent stopped
inside the culvert bearing the brook west under the road
a large metal pipe that amplified the dog's whimpers and moans
dog of righteousness dog of retribution

we heard it from our house where soon the shutters would go up
we sat in the kitchen the summer air soft as a damp rag we knew
this was a moment of consequence but we couldn't tell
whether the world had grown larger or smaller

Moles

where is his hat where is his horse where is his harrier my belovèd
is distraught he made this yard each blade each stem each stalk except
the mounds of fresh dirt like little graves it's moles that make the mounds
when they make holes they're worms with fur the cat

does not do moles she's stalking rooks and mice belovèd
has scattered human hair across the sod it keeps the deer away
he has installed a high-pitched hum in the lily bed it keeps the dogs
out of the yard who might have otherwise unearthed a mole too bad

traps don't work the way they do for squirrels my father
used to thrust the hose into one hole and flood them out my belovèd
does not care what my father did this greensward is his joy his job
my job was children food house the rest of what I did stayed underground

Garter Snake

hibernaculum a hole in the earth
from which in spring the snakes ooze forth the males
much smaller than the female stretched out like a tree-limb
among the tulips not moving not rippling or flinching preoccupied
a film over her eyes along her body the smaller snakes
flex and extend they may be helping her shed or may be
roughhousing like little boys which is what I thought at the pond
when I saw three mallards jump another duck they stayed underwater
a very long time she never did resurface the female snake seems
oblivious sheathed in ribbons one of them shudders off
and shimmies toward the lilac hedge our friend
wants to show us he can catch a snake at the top of its spine
and reaches into the grass but even a garter snake
has teeth we see it flung then reinvented half erect
on its coils hissing or taking soundings with its tongue
swiveling its head to follow the enemy
that's us

Groundhog

not unlike otters which we love frolicking
floating on their backs like truant boys unwrapping lunch
same sleek brown pelt some overtones of gray and rust
though groundhogs have no swimming hole and lunch
is rooted in the ground beneath short legs small feet
like a fat man's odd diminutive loafers not

frolicking but scurrying layers of fat his coat
gleams as though wet shines chestnut sable darker
head and muzzle lower into the grass a dark
triangular face like the hog-nosed skunk another delicate
nose and not a snout doesn't it matter what they're called I like swine

which are smart and prefer to be clean using their snouts
to push their excrement to the side of the pen
but they have hairy skin not fur his fur
shimmers and ripples he never uproots the mother plant his teeth
I think are blunt squared off like a sheep's if cornered does he
cower like sheep or bite like a sow with a litter is he ever

attacked he looks to me inedible he shares his acreage
with moles voles ravenous crows someone thought up
the names his other name is botched Algonquin but yes
he burrows beneath the barn where once a farmer

dried cordwood he scuttles there at speech cough laugh
at lawnmower swollen brook high wind he lifts his head
as Gandhi did small tilt to the side or stands erect
like a prairie dog or a circus dog but dogs don't waddle like Mao

with a tiny tail he seems asexual like Gandhi like Jesus if Jesus
came back would he be vegetarian also pinko freako homo

in Vermont natives scornful of greyhounds from the city
self-appoint themselves woodchucks unkempt hairy macho
who would shoot on sight an actual fatso shy mild marmot radiant
as the hog-nosed skunk in the squirrel trap both cleaner than sheep
fur fluffy like a girl's maybe he is a she it matters
what we're called words shape the thought don't say
rodent and ruin everything

Hog-Nosed Skunk

because she's half blind and thus prefers
complete not partial darkness and because
she cannot raise her tail entirely over her back
in order to use her one weapon her one defense
when you come to the squirrel trap from behind
and cover with a blanket the wire box
although my belovèd won't believe it
she just gives up she just gives up

Hound

since thought is prayer if hard and true I thought that thought
could lead me to compassion for my fellow creatures
insects excluded contrary to the Buddha I swat them dead
the wasps might show a little compassion too I do include
the hound next door it moans all day all night
a loud slow lament a child can make itself sustain

to dramatize its misery this dog was once
the neighbors' child but now they have an actual child
he's been cast down to be a dog again chained outdoors heartsick
uncomprehending why can't he just buck up remember his roots his lot
not more special than any other
                          sad hound look up
at the fledglings' wide mouths look over here
at the cat teaching her litter how to hunt all sleek all black
they're interchangeable her many tits confirm no favorites
no first no last
                    at least with only two
both can be a kind of favorite it's better than three
I ought to know my sister and I each had one parent to herself
like Tea for Two it wasn't hard to be the boy
until there came the actual boy he was nothing like my father
what does it mean to have flown from the same nest into the world
you're thinking one is best
                                one open mouth no first no last but isn't it
then the parents who compete no wonder the father of animals
wanders off the best is two all right one parent and one child
we've seen it work among the elephants

Lost Boy

who says we aren't primarily animals for instance
you recognize at once the smell of doom and keep away unless
you're drawn by pheromones like a soldier ant or for once you worry
about your soul he reeked of doom despised by those he loved one parent
missing one parent Pentecostal disgusted by the queer parts of him
he was himself disgusted self-despising snarling sick

unto death the chronic contagious sickness of our times
a righteous judgment was what he called it the rash
erupted over and over no meds no money no readiness
for help if there'd been help no self-defense unless you count
self-sabotage the wounds were old and ugly he kept them fresh he was quick
to take offense except from me and for what for merely a kindness

that brought me letters photos poems seeds saved from his yard roses
profuse on the cards for Mother's Day on valentines because I was a surrogate
it cost me nothing until he chose oblivion the news was no surprise his gift
was always making something out of nothing

Maestro

he smoked like a chimney we used to say unfiltered
Chesterfields the fragile horizontal column of ash
lengthening as he winced at the sour notes but plunged ahead
even when it splashed down onto the keyboard his long hands
showing the smaller hands how it was done the Chopin the Bach
or some reduction of the Nutcracker Suite whatever might be needed
in order to teach the young you also need

herculean belief in the possible and his had sugared off
into a pure elixir he must have sipped from
nights in his rented room in the widow's house I suppose
she cooked for him and always someone's mother had sent pie
everyone knew it wasn't us he loved
but he made his Chevrolet an open closet instruments and scores
and the book that conjured every known song
when there were two pianos the two of us

took turns the solo the orchestra imagine
the odds that he'd turn up in my life in time
to loosen the bony grip of Mrs. Law who kept
the ledger of your mistakes and whose breath could peel back bark
exactly as my older sister said when she leapt from the bench
and fled the lessons leaving me behind it didn't matter
whether I was worthy or unworthy he took me
everywhere in the Chevrolet he played
with flat fingers I do too

Geese

there is no cure for temperament it's how
we recognize ourselves but sometimes within it
a narrowing imprisons or is opened such as when my mother
in her last illness snarled and spat and how this lifted my dour father
into a patient tenderness thereby astounding everyone
but mostly it hardens who we always were

if you've been let's say a glass-half-empty kind of girl
you wake to the chorus of geese overhead
forlorn for something has softened their nasal voices
their ugly aggression on the ground they're worse than chickens
but flying one leader falling back another moving up to pierce the wind
no one in charge or every one in charge in flight each limited goose
adjusts its part in the cluster just under the clouds
do they mean together to duplicate the cloud
like the pelicans on the pond rearranging their shadows
to fool the fish another collective that constantly recalibrates but fish
don't need to reinvent themselves the way geese do
when they negotiate the sky
                              on the fixed
unyielding ground there is no end to hierarchy
the flock the pack the family you know it's true if you're
a take-charge kind of girl I recommend
houseplants in the windows facing south
the cacti the cyclamen are blooming on the brink
of winter all it took was a little enforced deprivation
a little premature and structured dark

Birch

before it's too late I need to study the great religions time
is speeding up in the bad movie of my life months fly off
the calendar or the camera stays fixed on one tree
in leaf no leaves in leaf sunrise sunset
as the great Yiddish musical says

and then the *chuppah* the goblet smashed delirious dancers
parading the newlyweds in chairs like royalty but why
give up those beasts whose hooves leave valentines
for us in the muddy sty and why so much anxiety
regarding women ditto Mary's
beatific smile but I like distinctive hats on those in charge
and I know I need a little intercession spilt salt
flung over the shoulder a daily lineup facing east
though some of us have to pray in our personal tents
like snails
          a wedding in a garden
suits me fine the flowers left unsacrificed
it's Adam and Eve except that Adam had no mother
no one who worried about that missing rib now incarnate
wearing white like a young birch beside my boy who's grown
bewitched looking nowhere but at her I know that look
a Druid with his chosen tree he might as well
be on his knees he needs an altar something old something
once revered perhaps I could volunteer bring on the saw the guests
can bow their heads and count the rings the years

Bear

pressed full-length against the screen unzipping it
for a better grip to help him help himself to the seed and the suet
slung high under the eave by the man
who has charged down from the bedroom onto the porch
in his white loincloth like David against Goliath
but only one good lung shouting swearing
and behind him the woman caught
at the lip of the lit kitchen
                            where was my sister
with her gun or would she be praying since she prays routinely
for a parking spot and there it is or would she be speechless for once
that this man so moderate so genial so unlike me
had put himself one body-length away from a full-grown bear
or would she be saying you my dear are the person who married him
which of course I did I did and I stood behind him
as he stood his ground on the ground that is our porch
                                    you can see
the marks gouged by the famous claws on the wall inside new screen
now laced by a wire trellis on which nothing climbs
a vertical electric fence one of us thinks
the bear can hear it hum from the edge of the woods
watching us like a child sent to his room as we grill the salmon
we spiked with juniper berries the other one thinks
the plural pronoun is a dangerous fiction the source
of so much unexpected loneliness

Chameleon

beside myself in Texas the doctors asking my belovèd
to give his pain a number one to ten his answer is always
two I tell them eight the holly bush in the yard is putting out new leaves
which makes its resident lizard bright green also light brown
along its slender spine a plausible twig
except the lining of its mouth is red as it puts away
in three quick bites some kind of fly and then at its throat
a rosy translucent sac swells and subsides maybe peristaltic
pushing its meal forward or maybe preening for a mate or maybe
residual from the blooming hibiscus shrub or maybe learned from frogs
that also live in a tree but singing is dangerous if you mean
to replicate vegetation
                    O exquisite creature
whose dull cousin back in Vermont the brown lizard
navigates our dooryard by alternating pairs of elbows like oars
determined and clumsy moving across the gravel yet moving forward
I see you do not move unless you need to eat you almost fool
the mockingbird nearby in a live oak tree flinging out another's song
which is me which which is me

Lament

absence neither sweet nor bitter
without the aftertaste of willfulness does it happen
as the dipper fixed in the northern sky turns
to lie on its side no longer facing east
where in late summer the bull rises with its bright red eye

or is it more like a rock in the swollen stream millennia
to bind its layered parts then battered cleaved
then one half tumbled away

idiopathic is what they say to say
no evident cause no trigger no blame except to blame
the way the world winds down winds up again shifting particles
as easily as pollen in the wind

stars stone lichen glued to the stone a human hand

and so one hand withdrawn from the other hand
what had been paired a left a right
                                            every cell divides
in order to multiply it's where we began

Spring

years of unearthing the rocks out of the field and soon enough
you've built a stone wall the longer the marriage

the less the need for trying to agree but we've agreed
what will happen at the end of it nothing

except the old immutable forms
like a shovel shared at the grave for texts

Ecclesiastes so the bereaved
can choose whether to believe

that death is a kind of hibernation this spring the groundhog
foraging in our yard was smaller thinner a strange

perpendicular crimp in its tail which proved
to the rational mind it was a different creature but look belovèd

how by late summer it's fattened out how its coat now gleams how
when frightened it also hurries into the barn

Sleep

another heavy frost what doesn't die or fly away
the groundhog for instance the bear is deep in sleep I'm thinking
a lot about sleep translation I'm not sleeping much
who used to be a champion of sleep
ex-champions are pathetic my inner parent says the world
is full of evil death cruelty degradation not sleeping
scores only 2 out of 10
                         but a moral sense
is exhausting I am exhausted a coma looks good to me
if only I could be sure there'd still be dreams it's what I miss the most
even in terrible dreams at least you feel what you feel not what
you're supposed to feel your house burns down so what
if you survived you rake the ashes sobbing
                             exhausted
from trying to not smoke I once asked for a simple errand
from my belovèd who wanted me not to smoke he forgot unforgivable
I fled the house like an animal wounded enraged I was thinking
more clearly than I had ever thought my thought was why

prolong this life I flung myself into the car I drove like a fiend
to the nearest store I asked unthinking for unfiltered Luckies oh
brand of my girlhood I paid the price I took my prize to the car I slit
the cellophane I tapped out one perfect white cylinder I brought to my face
the smell of the barns the fires that cooked it golden brown smell of my father
my uncles my grandfather's tin of loose tobacco his packet of delicate paper
the deliberate way he rolled and licked and tapped and lit and drew in
and relished it the smell of the wild girls behind the gym the boys
in pickup trucks I sat in my car as the other cars crept by
I looked like a pervert it was perverse

a Lucky under my nose
                    I drove myself home
I threw away the pack which was unwise the gods
don't notice whining they notice the brief bright flares of human will
they lean from their couches yes more fear and dread for that one
yes let's turn the suffering up a notch let's watch her
strike the match I strike it now when I wake
in the dark I light that little fire

Larch

short-sleeves in Vermont late November the leaves long gone
only evergreens the white birch bark and our feral black cat
not sheltering prowling improbably in her thickened coat
one more free-range lunch one more of her nine lives
put back into reserve unlike the year's fresh deaths

as for me I keep my votive candles burning as the larches burned
on the hillside their needles yellow deciduous like the leaves
and now sloughed in the yard beneath the small larch
bent double cascading like a willow weeping is the proper name for it
also for the cherry tree in the yard of the house where my parents' friend
shot an intruder it was his wife their tree

might as well be here with all my other lost trees childhood mimosas
magnolias the willow oak blown down in a storm surviving in my head
beside the friend the murdered wife the subsequent wife
my parents too and now Peter with his lazy eye and glamorous
doom-ridden Rynn and Carol who had her own reprieves

who used them up I confess the weather matters more and more to me
diurnal is a lovely word another is circadian

Roof

after a week of daily heavy snow I want to praise my roof first
the acute angle at which it descends from the ridgepole
and second that it is black the color absorbing
all the other colors so that even now as arctic air
blows in from the plains my roof burns off from underneath
the dazzling snow dense layers of particles which are tiny
specks of trash sheathed in wet cloud what chance
do they have against my roof even at night
the snowpack over my head breaks apart and slides on its own melting
down from the eaves as though my roof had shrugged I hear snow
thump to the ground a cleansing sound the secret of my roof
is standing seams the raised ridges
bonding the separate panels to one another an old
wound that has healed no lapped shingles catching the wind
no icejam at the eaves no sending my belovèd out with an ax
no roof caved in from the weight of snow as happened in 1924 only
another thump as a slab of snow lets loose leaving my roof
gleaming in the wet residue it takes what it needs
from the lifesource and sheds the rest a useful
example if I were starting over

Storm

one minute a slender pine indistinguishable from the others
the next its trunk horizontal still green the jagged stump
a nest for the flickers
                              one minute high wind and rain the skies
lit up the next a few bright winking stars the lashing of the brook

one minute an exaltation in the apple trees the shadblow trees
the next white trash on the ground new birds
or the same birds crowding the feeder
one minute the children were sleeping in their beds

you got sick you got well you got sick

the lilac bush we planted is a tree the cat creeps past
with something in her mouth she's hurrying down to where

the culvert overflowed one minute bright yellow
marsh marigolds springing up the next
the farmer sweeps them into his bales of hay

ACKNOWLEDGMENTS

Claiming Kin, copyright 1976 by Ellen Bryant Voigt. Used with permission of Wesleyan University Press.

A number of poems in this volume have been revised since their initial publication in magazines and books. The arrangement of poems in *Two Trees* differs significantly from the arrangement in the first edition.

I am ever grateful for the help that Catherine Barnett, Andrea Barrett, Katherine Branch, Michael Collier, David Lanier, and Dudley Voigt provided in the preparation of this manuscript.

Thanks for the generous support from the National Endowment for the Arts, the John Simon Guggenheim Memorial Foundation, the Rockefeller Foundation, and the John D. and Catherine T. MacArthur Foundation, which enabled many of these poems.

I want also to acknowledge poets whose work prompted or enabled some of these poems: Stephen Dobyns (the narratives in *The Lotus Flowers*), Agha Shahid Ali ("Himalaya"), Sandy McClatchy (the translations of Horace). Larry Levis ("What I Remember of Larry's Dream of Yeats"),

Reg Gibbons and Michael Ryan ("Rubato"), Carl Phillips ("Redbud"), Michael Collier ("The Feeder"). Tony Hoagland ("Cow") and Jim Longenbach ("Privet Hedge").

I have been fortunate to have had the support of numerous editors of journals and magazines over the years. Also, at W. W. Norton: editors Kathleen Anderson, Carol Houck Smith, and Jill Bialosky; assistant editor Drew Weitman; senior editor Amy Cherry; and publisher Drake McFeely.

Finally, my deep gratitude for the acute, candid, instructive responses I have received from generous readers over the years—many of them my colleagues in the Warren Wilson MFA Program for Writers.

DEDICATIONS

Claiming Kin
"The Heart Is the Target," Louise
"Dialogue: Poetics," Paul Nelson
"Birthday Sestina," Ola Dudley Yeatts

The Forces of Plenty
"A Fugue," Tom Moore, M.D.
"Epithalamium," Keith

Two Trees
"Effort at Speech," William Meredith
"Song and Story," Allen Grossman

Kyrie
"Girls adore their teacher . . . ," Marge Sable

Shadow of Heaven
"Practice," Steve Orlen
"The Art of Distance, 4," Fran
"Dooryard Flower," in memory of Tom Moore, M.D.

NOTES

72   *"The long habit of living / indisposes us to dying"* ("A Fugue"): A paraphrase from Sir Thomas Browne.

107   *"But if she has eaten the food of the dead, / she cannot wholly return to the upper air."* ("Rescue"): From Ovid.

149   *"Women, women, what do they want?"* ("The Wide and Varied World"): A paraphrase from Sigmund Freud.

193   *"Having stolen twelve of Apollo's cows / he butchered two: an offering to the gods, / and one for himself, since he was hungry."* ("First Song"): From the "Homeric Hymn to Hermes."

243   "Kyrie ('kir-ē-,ā)" (*Kyrie*): "A short liturgical prayer that begins with or consists of the words 'Lord, have mercy.'" *Merriam-Webster's Online Dictionary*: https://www.merriam-webster.com/dictionary/kyrie.

390   *"on whom nothing is lost."* ("The Hive"): Henry James, *The Art of Fiction*.

INDEX OF TITLES

INDEX OF FIRST LINES

one minute a slender pine indistinguishable from the others   454
One-third of the house is hanging in the air,   168
Our two children grown, now   315

pressed full-length against the screen unzipping it   446
Put this in your notebooks: 127

Raccoons on the porch, the deer   187
rangy loping swiveling left then right I'm thinking   434
Reading in bed, full of sentiment   116

She completes the generic oval, a feathered   206
She has come next door to practice our piano.   30
She looked at my hand as into a bowl of soup;   224
She sits at the table   52
short-sleeves in Vermont late November the leaves long gone   452
Since morning they have been quarreling—   99
since thought is prayer if hard and true I thought that thought   441
Slender, cylindrical,   209
Snow heaped like a hat, square gray face,   267
So few birds—the ones that winter through   167
Soft *chink*—   53
Something was killing sheep   137
Stringy, skittery, thistle-burred, rib-etched,   392
Swarming over the damp ground with pocket lenses   117
Sweet are the songs of bitterness and blame,   276

Thanksgiving Day was the day they slaughtered the hog the carcass   432
"The accident" is what he called the time   188
The afternoon spreads its fingers on the lawn,   63
The almost visible wall   199
The barber, the teacher, the plumber, the preacher,   271
The body, a resonant bowl: 71

Who could remember cause? Both   56
Who said the worst was past, who knew   286
who says we aren't primarily animals for instance   442
Whoever said that I should count on mind?   366
Why did you have to go back, go back   303
With no more coffins left, why not one wagon   284
Wrinkle coming toward me in the grass—no,   341

years of unearthing the rocks out of the field and soon enough   449
You cannot see the horns from where you sit,   134
You were a man with only your own resources,   55
You wiped a fever-brow, you burned the cloth.   268